The Intrepid Wanderer's Guide To Ancient Egyptian Goddesses

The Intrepid Wanderer's Guide to Ancient Egyptian Goddesses

Written and Illustrated by Zachary Gray

The Intrepid Wanderer's Guide to Ancient Egyptian Goddesses

Intrepid Spirit Books

Book and cover design by Intrepid Spirit Books
Printed in the United States of America

www.talkancientegypt.blogspot.com

ISBN-978-0-615-25880-5

This book is dedicated to everyone who has ever wandered with me

Author's Preface

My endless fascination with ancient Egypt began in the fertile imagination of childhood. Over the years, this fire has been fueled by an abundance of exhibitions around the world, the wealth of information to be found in research, and most of all by spending time in Egypt—exploring the ancient monuments, lingering in the shadows of majestic columned halls, and deciphering the revelatory inscriptions on temple walls. In recent years I wondered what I, as an intrepid wanderer, could do to pay this not-entirely-vanished culture fitting gratitude for all of the investigative pleasure and inspiration received.

This book is one answer.

In ***The Intrepid Wanderer's Guide to Ancient Egyptian Goddesses,*** I have attempted to elucidate an aspect of the most important dimension of ancient Egyptian culture: the religious dimension. Gods, goddesses, and cult temples gave the Egyptians as much *raison d'etre* as the Nile itself and with this glorious river these divinities and their sanctuaries were most intimately bound. While the full scope of ancient Egyptian cosmology, folklore, and religious practice is far too sweeping and complex to be captured within the framework of any one book, it is my desire to give the reader an informative and entertaining glimpse of Egypt's magnificent goddesses.

Though Egyptologists (to whom we Egyptophiles are forever indebted) rightly point out that the primary building projects and military campaigns of the united "Two Lands" were usually carried out under the patronage of male deities, it was often the goddesses who sustained the workaday spiritual and economic pulse of the people. It was also the goddesses who lasted until the bitter end, when authentic Egyptian religious tradition was but a shred of memory. Make no mistake about it: ancient Egyptian goddesses were an impressive lot. Their value, at least from an approach of the study of Humanities, far exceeds the obvious allure of their breathtaking sensuality and primordial fecundity. Egyptian goddesses were long-suffering, hard-working, crafty (when they had to be), deadpan, powerful, mischievous, and, above all, *magical.* Whether navigating the treacherous waters of the Underworld or harpooning malevolent hippos, Egyptian goddesses boasted a workload that would likely wilt the divine dames of Greece and Rome.

All of the truly great goddesses of Egypt are featured in this book—Isis, Hathor, Mut, Neith, Sekhmet, Wadjet, etc.—along with detailed information about their roles in ancient theological systems and popular thought. Though the author is an avid researcher, rather than an Egyptologist, some of the most respected and hard-to-find scientific sources have been investigated to create individual accounts of the goddesses that are both revealing and accessible. Everyone excited about ancient Egypt is free to explore the panorama of diverse scholarly information and draw conclusions according to their own intelligence and ability. While we would be lost without the hard-working scientists of Egyptology, it is crucial to remember that the study of ancient Egypt is a legacy belonging to the entire world, and not solely to an elite few. So much of the pertinent information available can indeed be understood and appreciated by *so many* of all backgrounds. It is my wish that the entries in this book will inspire those investigating the wonder and mystery of ancient Egyptian religion to dig deeper with the scholars—as I did—in their own explorations.

Though it may help to have a foundational knowledge of ancient Egyptian religious themes to enjoy this book, it is not necessary. The emphasis here is upon the unique history and various qualities of each included goddess. Also, a number of sections at the beginning and end of the work touch upon temple design, daily cult, cult centers, maps, and original photographs.

The world's widespread fascination with ancient Egypt never seems to go out of style and if you, too, are fortunate enough to visit that beautiful land and its temples one day, this guide may prove helpful. Even in times of political uncertainty, Egypt remains a safe and welcoming nation, in this writer's experience. Always consult a well-respected travel agent and licensed guideperson about the possibilities of making your own once-in-a-lifetime journey to the realm of the ancient pharaohs. Whether you're a genuine Egyptophile or merely an intrepid wanderer, you'll be glad you did.

Important Points to Ponder Before Reading

It is valuable to remember that the ancient Egyptians were very comfortable blending the attributes and qualities of their various gods and goddesses. The reader will note that many goddesses often shared the same mythological traditions and adventures, but this was never confusing to the Egyptians, who regarded plurality as a normal feature of their general religious understanding. In this sense, an obscure local or "neighborhood" goddess could be easily regarded as the local manifestation of a greater, national goddess like Isis or Mut.

This fusion of characteristics is sometimes called *syncretism* and demonstrates the open attitude the Egyptians possessed toward the multi-dimensional personification of divine forces that were only somewhat beyond their control. The ancient Egyptians did indeed believe that their deities could be controlled (to a certain extent) by the constant maintenance of temple rituals overseen by their priests, who acted as representatives of the one true priest: Pharaoh. This underscores the attempt by the ancients to understand these forces and "mysteries" on an everyday level.

Important Time Periods Covered in this Book

Numerous Dynastic time-periods, specific pharaohs, and occupational rulers are often mentioned in this book. The basic information below can be useful for the reader who is interested in quickly cross-referencing goddesses and various epochs mentioned in their particular regard. Dates specific to individual Dynasties and monarchs will be noted in the text of the book when pertinent.

Pre-Dynastic Periods (Before 2660 BCE)

Old Kingdom (2660-2180 BCE)

Middle Kingdom (2080-1640 BCE)

New Kingdom (1570-1075 BCE)

The Late Period (712-332 BCE)

Ptolemaic Period (332-30 BCE)

Roman Period (30 BCE-640 CE)

A Day in the Life of an Egyptian Temple

Quite unlike our modern houses of worship, the ancient Egyptian temple was considered to be both the "house" of a particular deity and a carefully constructed, magically charged "device" intended to enact and maintain a cosmological balance between the visible world and the abode of the gods and goddesses. Every aspect of the temple served to achieve this goal by virtue of architectural design (often to the smallest detail) and the unique sequence of inscriptions adorning walls, columns, and sanctuaries. Though the earliest Egyptian temples were little more than reed huts marked by a flagpole and a deity's unique totem, the temple evolved into a relatively standard form by the coming of the late Middle Kingdom Period.

Surrounded by a large mud-brick enclosure wall thought to symbolize the rippling "primordial waters of creation," the brick, limestone, or granite interiors of an Egyptian goddess's "house" were generally off-limits to everyone except her priests, the Pharaoh, and select members of the noble class. Open courtyards led progressively to a Hypostyle Hall and then to the innermost sanctuary, where a suite of chapels housed the *naos* (or shrine) of the chief deity and sometimes those of associated gods. There were also myriad rooms used for the deitiy's sacred Bark, religious supplies, administrative offices, and sacrificial preparation areas (kitchens and butcheries).

Hierarchical personnel serving in "phyles," or rotational shifts, comprised the staff of most Egyptian temples. Priests were almost always male, except in the early Dynasties, when priestesses are attested—especially for goddesses like Hathor and Neith. Chief among the priests were the "Prophets" (*Hem-Netjer*) of the gods. These individuals often directly oversaw or delegated administration of the temple economy, festivals, property holdings, livestock, and treasury—all of which could be crucial to both temple and community economy. Their main responsibility, however, was the care and nurturing of the chief cult-statue housed in any given temple. It was the prophet of the resident god that had almost exclusive access to the Holy of Holies sanctuary for performance of the thrice-daily rites.

These rites typically began with the opening of the shrine's cabinet-like doors, a greeting and "awakening" of the deity, anointing with precious oils and unguents, the burning of incense, singing of hymns, changing of garments on the sacred image, and the offering of various foodstuffs. Ritual purity was of the utmost importance, and prophets were required to shave their bodies and perform sacred ablutions before entering the Holy of Holies. To assist them in these preparatory functions and other tasks were lesser priests called *wab* (or "pure") priests. These priests generally operated in the aforementioned phyles or "rotating teams" to ensure the upkeep of the temple's day-to-day routine and the wider prerogatives of the various cult-gods within.

Finally, scribes, cooks, lectors, singers, and dancers were among the various other types of personnel employed by the temple, depending upon its size, wealth, and the importance of the resident divinity.

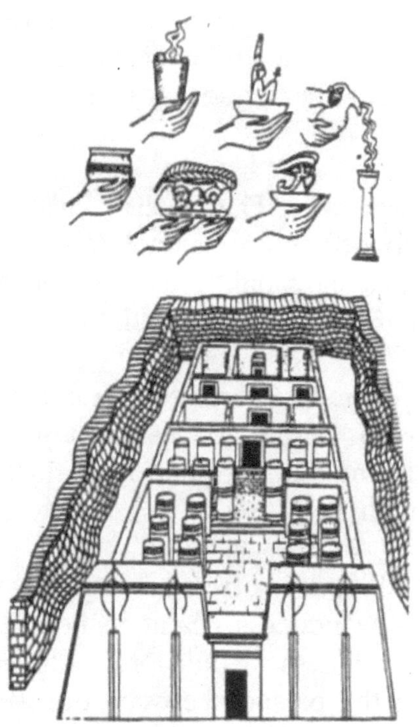

Some Ritual Items Offered *Especially* to Egyptian Goddesses

In addition to incense, wine, and food offerings, special gifts were offered to the goddess of a particular temple. It is important to understand that whatever Pharaoh himself "gave" to the goddess (and Pharaoh was always considered to be the universal, ultimate High Priest), he expected to receive as a gift from *her* in return. Here are some of the more unique offerings that could be extended to the Chief Goddess and her associates in any given sanctuary.

The Clepsydra This ancient "water-clock" was usually offered by Pharaoh to a goddess in the hope that she would grant him longevity of life and dominion over the land.

Censer Pharaoh offered this extended device to the nostrils of the goddess in hope that the scent of resins burning upon its surface would be pleasing to her.

Ma'at Pharaoh offered to goddesses the image of the goddess Ma'at in hope that the *recipient* goddess would reward him by preserving the balance between the worlds of chaos and order. Obviously, this was a crucial rite for the good of the kingdom as a whole.

Menat Collar This royal "collar" was beaded and, when shaken, made a shimmering sound that was thought to be especially pleasing to the ears of a goddess.

Sistrum This sacred rattle was shaken before a great many goddesses as part of daily ritual, but especially for goddesses who could sometimes be ferocious by nature, and who required some extra "pacification." The sound of the rattle was thought to soothe their foul moods. The sistrum was especially sacred to Hathor, Isis, Sekhmet, Mut, Nephthys, Bastet, and the very ancient goddess Bat.

Udjat Eye The sacred Eye of Horus (the son of Isis and Osiris) was offered as a sign of the magical protection and unified, all-seeing "power" which the Pharaoh expected as a gift from the recipient goddess.

Enneads, Ogdoads, Triads, and Dyads

Throughout this book, the reader will encounter various groups of deities collectively known as Enneads, Ogdoads, Triads, and Dyads. It should be noted that almost every Egyptian locality had its own, often modified, version of universal creation that corresponded to the "official" versions elaborated by theologians in major religious centers like Thebes, Heliopolis, Memphis, or Sais. Everywhere, temple priesthoods often preferred to gather resident gods in groups that reflected local traditions, theological concepts, and needs particular to the community. The magical power inherent in names and numbers were of great significance to the ancient Egyptians and, for this reason, towns usually honored an Ennead, or group of nine "primary" gods. Often, the number of deities would far exceed the traditional nine, but the collective was still described as an Ennead.

Enneads

The local Ennead of any Egyptian town was generally patterned after the "Great Ennead" of Heliopolis—a cosmic family of gods consisting of Atum-Ra, Shu, Tefnut, Geb, Nut, Osiris, Set, Isis, Nephthys (and sometimes Haroeris). The members of this Great Ennead were recipients of a sort of honorary cult throughout Egypt during most time periods. As noted, individual towns did construct their *own* deity groups, but these were usually considered "Lesser Enneads" out of deference to the Great Ennead of Heliopolis. Readers will learn much more about the deities of the Great Ennead as they read the goddess-entries throughout this book.

The Ogdoad

Another important grouping of Creator Gods was honored at the city of Hermopolis. Eight in number, this Ogdoad consisted of four male/female pairs representing various forces of Chaos in existence even before the solar system was “fashioned.” Nun and Naunet were the god and goddess of the waters present at the dawn of Eternity. Kuk and Kuket were gods who personified darkness. Amun and Amaunet personified the mysterious properties of invisibility. Huh and Huhet embodied the very concept of Eternity itself.

The ancient Egyptians believed that this Ogdoad used magic to form an island that emerged from primordial waters. Soon, an egg appeared on the island; from that egg was hatched the solar god Atum, or Ra (in his manifestation of the personality “Harakhte”). Though occasionally portrayed in temple iconography as screeching baboons greeting the first-ever rising of the sun, the members of the Ogdoad usually appeared as human forms, though the male gods had the faces of frogs while the goddesses had serpentine faces. Hermopolis or “Town of the Eight” (as it was called by the ancient Egyptians) was believed to be the actual site of the Sacred Island of the Ogdoad, but it is unclear whether this group of gods possessed an actual temple in which they received a ritual cult.

Rather, the “Tombs” of the Ogdoad members were venerated in Hermopolis, along with a relic believed to be a portion of the cosmic egg from which Atum-Ra was born. Due to the Ogdoad’s rather abstract qualities, Pharaohs were not exactly clamoring to honor them with sanctuaries; remember that the Ogdoad represented forces occurring at the *dawn* of

Time—forces that often did not seem to have the same kind of immediate relevance to daily life along the Nile as did other deities. Only in the later periods of Egyptian history did members of the Ogdoad become recipients of a peculiar collective worship, especially on certain Festival Days in the temples at Dendera and Edfu.

The Triad

Most ancient Egyptian towns honored either a supreme god (or goddess) and usually paired their resident male god with a chief female deity in a relationship not to be considered quite equal to the Western concept of marriage. Rather, these deities were allied more as companions or consorts. Eventually, with the rise of New Kingdom Egypt, more definitive "family" structures were tailored for gods and the normative, local temple was generally inhabited by a male god as "husband," a goddess as "wife," and a third god—usually another local male god "adopted" by the couple—was co-opted into their temple and rendered in child-form. Examples of renowned Egyptian triads include Osiris-Isis-Horus, Amun-Mut-Khons, Ptah-Sekhmet-Nefertum, and Khnum-Satis-Anukis.

The Dyad

Occasionally, local deities would be paired-up due to similar (or sometimes quite polarized) characteristics; ancient Egyptians were fascinated with dualities. Deities could also be paired due to some mythological or ritual association that had particular significance for a certain community. Examples of famous dyads were Horus-Anti at Qau al-Kebir, Hathor-Nekhbet of El Kab, Isis-Renenutet of the Fayyum, Anukis-Nephthys of Komir, and Hathor-Sekhmet of Imaou.

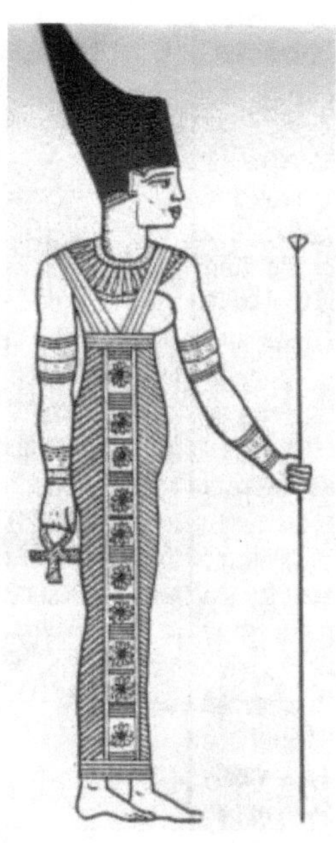

Amaunet

Primary Role: Consort of Amun and Nursing-Mother of the Pharaoh
Chief Title: "Mistress of Both Countries"
Cult Centers: Karnak/Thebes

It is a pity that ancient Egyptian mythology harbored no concept of formal divorce between a male deity and his consort. If the ancients *had* appreciated the nuances of this scenario, the goddess Amaunet might not have been exiled into relative obscurity, the bane of every immortal.

Amaunet's career as a goddess is rather enigmatic. There's a strong chance that she was simply "manufactured" in the early dynastic periods to provide a consort for the god Amun in his primordial manifestation. Although Amaunet's name is an obvious feminization of her husband's title (meaning "The Hidden One"), she was not exactly a mere shadow. Indeed, Amaunet was the recipient of a specialized cult of her own for a substantial portion of ancient Egyptian history.

Much indeed has been debated about the origin of Amun, Amaunet, and the meaning of the title "Hidden One(s)." For some, this epithet exemplifies a role as the personification of invisibility, along with the impossibility of the human mind to know the true essence of all that is mysterious or beyond explanation. It should be remembered that such abstruse concepts often had complex primordial/cosmic overtones in Egyptian theology. Knowing this, it is no surprise to learn that Amaunet's early association with Amun secured a place for her—at Amun's side—as one of the eight creative forces that formed the Ogdoad of Hermopolis. Therein, the goddess could be portrayed with the head of a serpent and feet like the heads of jackals. (For more about the Ogdoad, see the preceding section on Enneads, Ogdoads, Triads, and Dyads).

Quite apart from her apparent presence within the Ogdoad, Amaunet would become a distinctly cosmopolitan goddess at Thebes, after the cult of Amun made its definitive appearance there in the years leading up to the reign of Pharaoh Amenemhet I in Dynasty XII (1991-1962 BCE) during the Middle Kingdom. At that time, Amaunet may have joined her husband in human form on the walls of his initially modest temple. She may also have been the object of a statue-cult in that temple as well. Likely, when the priests of Amun completed the necessary rituals for the image of their chief god, lesser rites and leftover offerings were relegated to the image of his consort.

Royal "Mother Figure" in the Karnak Temple

When Middle Kingdom Pharaohs began to shift their political and religious alliances from the triumphal Theban war-god, Montu, they subsequently patronized the cult of Amun. As a result, Amun rose to enormous fame and fortune at Thebes, with Amaunet at his side. She appears to have inhabited the temple at Karnak as a mother-figure to Pharaoh, as well as being Amun's companion, from at least the time of Senwosret I (1965-1920 BCE). As a nursing-goddess, Amaunet was able to nurture Pharaoh to the level of strength required for his role as both uniter and lord of the Two Lands.

It is unclear whether Amaunet possessed her own temple independent from that of Amun, or if she even *needed* to possess one over the centuries. After all, Karnak's massive, constantly growing parameters afforded ample room for the auxiliary worship of many gods in Amun's sizeable entourage. More likely, Amaunet's statue seems to have dwelled in one (or perhaps several) of the small lateral chambers near the central sanctuary of her consort. Nevertheless, Amaunet did possess her very own retinue of "prophets," so the existence of a more tailored and impressive sanctuary for this goddess, somewhere in the vast expanse of Karnak, cannot be entirely ruled-out. Indeed, based upon evidence from Dynasty XVII (before 1539 BCE), it appears that Amaunet's cult-statue could be tended by perhaps a dozen personnel at any given time. This indicates that her worship was subsidiary but not necessarily minor; her name and imagery were scattered throughout the temples of Karnak and Luxor, even into the later periods of ancient Egyptian history. The goddess should not be underestimated.

Amaunet—A Form of Neith?

In temple reliefs at Thebes, Amaunet was usually adorned with the Red Crown of Lower Egypt. This indicates that her origins were, in some way, connected with the northern portion of the kingdom. To be certain, regardless of her presence in the Ogdoad of Hermopolis, Amaunet *is* first mentioned in the Heliopolitan Dynasty V Pyramid Texts as a protectress of Pharaoh, along with Amun. The presence of the Red Crown in Amaunet's iconography has also led some to believe that she was, at the outset, a mere alternative form of the powerful goddess Neith, of Sais. There is late inscriptional evidence of a syncretistic kinship between these two goddesses at Thebes, but scholars have thus far been unable to fully elucidate the extent or antiquity of this association.

Though Amaunet was perhaps perceived by some late ancient Egyptian priests as a stylized form of Neith, she certainly never enjoyed the mythical or cultic independence that Neith was able to command. Even so, being the consort of Amun was not a throwaway role; this status enabled Amaunet to be portrayed on temple walls as a prominent figure in Pharaoh's Jubilee or "Sed" Festival and she was honored with the title "Mistress of Both Countries"—a nod to her status as partner of the god who utterly ruled the Two Lands which formed the whole of ancient Egypt.

Another Goddess on the Horizon

Curiously, after the Middle Kingdom, Amaunet's primacy as consort of Amun at Thebes seems to have dimmed considerably because of growing alliances between the Temple of Amun and the cult of the goddess Mut, who was perhaps a specialized (or "local") form of the southern vulture-goddess, Nekhbet, and the great Memphite goddess, Sekhmet, who was generally depicted as a lioness. Though not much is known of Mut's exact origin, it appears that she was a popular goddess of the rural village of Megen, at some stage introduced to Thebes with sparkling results. Though Amaunet takes priority over Mut in certain early inscriptions where both goddesses are mentioned as associates of Amun (e.g. in the bark-chapel of Thutmose III), Mut was a goddess who most certainly came to possess a temple or "house" of her own in the city, unlike Amaunet.

Through the alliance of economic and cultic relations between the burgeoning Amun and Mut priesthoods, the figure of Mut was gradually brought with greater prominence into the god's entourage as the New Kingdom rolled into high-gear. It is possible that Amaunet, with her Lower Egyptian Red Crown, represented a kind of northern counterpoint to Mut, who came to personify the more dominant (and southern) female associate of Amun in his great city. In this sense, the two goddesses may have been viewed as companions of Amun appearing as Theban variants of Wadjet and Nekhbet, the official tutelary (or "crown") goddesses of Pharaonic Egypt. Eventually, the twosome of Amun and Mut took precedence and absorbed a local lunar deity, Khons, to form a triad.

These cultic consolidations aside, it is curious that Amun and Mut were rarely portrayed as a "couple" in temple inscriptions *without* the accompanying presence of Khons, perhaps out of respect for Amaunet's original prerogatives. Indeed, it is not entirely clear whether Mut was to be considered a consort, daughter, or political companion-goddess of

Amun. The case can be made that she played each of these roles. Whatever the reality, Amaunet always remained a genuine consort of Amun (or Amun-Ra), though she seems to have been curiously childless, save for her motherly duties to the king. This has also reinforced the belief of some researchers that Amaunet's intrinsic nature was, in truth, derived from that of the androgynous Neith of Sais, making her essentially sterile and thus untenable as a mother for Khons. Despite her noble attributes, Amaunet's one-time position as a chief goddess of Thebes (alongside Hathor and Opet) was decidedly eclipsed. Though Amaunet's cult-statue continued to receive attention and she continued to be depicted in temple reliefs well into the Greco-Roman period, this "Hidden One" faded into deeper shadows—her essentiality becoming "moot" with the arrival of...Mut.

REMNANTS OF AMAUNET: If the reader has the good fortune to one day visit the astonishing temple complexes of Karnak and Luxor in modern-day Thebes, the quiet but enduring personality of Amaunet can still be found, with a little detective work and the help of a knowledgeable guide.

Be certain to bring your camera to Karnak and ask your guide to point out the precinct known as the Record Hall of Thutmose III, who reigned in Dynasty XVIII. There, just beyond the Sixth Pylon of the great temple, the visitor will encounter a court housing a renowned statue of Amaunet, wearing her Red Crown, alongside her spouse. This partially ruined but sizeable image of the goddess appears to have been commissioned and modified (from an earlier sculpture) by none other than the famous "boy-king" himself, Tutankhamun.

If watchful, the intrepid traveler can behold exquisite reliefs of Amaunet throughout the Karnak and Luxor precincts, but most beautifully in the Festival Hall of Thutmose III at Karnak, just east of the Central Court. There, Amaunet and a host of other important Theban personalities lead a ritual procession in honor of the pharaoh's Jubilee celebration.

Bastet

Primary Role: Goddess of Pleasure and the Temperate Benefits of the Sun
Chief Title: "Eye of Ra," "Mistress of the City of Bast"
Cult Centers: Per-Bast (Bubastis), Saqqara

Picture, if you will, the sleek, sinewy form of a tawny feline, bathing itself in the heat of the Egyptian sun—a sun that sets over the walls of an ancient city in the Nile Delta. A balmy breeze glides through the tier-like streets, made refreshing by other zephyrs wafting from the Mediterranean. The cat's eyes blink in the knowing, satisfied fashion so common to its kind, reflecting the fade of solar rays in liquid plumes of fire. Its owner pauses to murmur some words of affection, perhaps giving a caress or two behind the ears. The cat simply blinks again and watches, forever "one" with the dwindling sun that comforts, the mystical city that shelters.

Far below, in the center of that city, a magnificent goddess dwells in a *naos* deep within her gorgeous temple. She makes no sound of her own, but one can imagine that she hears every breath and purr of her brood, every shimmer of the sacred sistrum rattle, and every accompanying prayer. The hundreds of felines dwelling in the city of Per-Bast yawn and curl into peaceful slumber. They have nothing to fear, for they are safe.

Bastet is watching!

Many modern people have at least a vague awareness that the domestic cat was considered especially holy to the ancient Egyptians. As cherished members of the household, cats were revered from early dynastic times, when they were valued for their ability to hunt rats, mice, snakes, and the various other pests which plagued human beings and their crops. Independent and seemingly "mysterious by design," cats strolled quite easily into the realm of popular Egyptian myth and theology. In fact, the great sun god Ra was often depicted as a He-Cat slaying the despicable cosmic serpent, Apophis. Once domesticated, cats were employed on the practical front to patrol Pharaoh's granaries in search of rapidly reproducing and destructive vermin. Sacred to the kings for this task alone, cats throughout Egypt could be viewed as property of Pharaoh "on loan" to host families who cared for the creatures. Or perhaps the host families were on loan to the cats, which often seems to be the attitude of cats across the world in our own time.

Though a number of ancient goddesses boasted feline attributes, Bastet generated most of the distinctly catty religious interest. Sleek and sensual, seductive and powerful, this was one of Egypt's primary independent goddesses, and one of the few never entirely defined by or subsidiary to the importance of any male consort. Though mythological construct could tout her readiness to rip Pharaoh's enemies to shreds (if she had to do so), this goddess was usually quite placid and more inclined to enjoy a rollicking party, as we shall see.

The Origin of Bastet

As is the case with most deities, it is somewhat difficult to discern the exact cultic origin of Bastet, much less her initial function. The hieroglyphic signs that form her name feature a container used for healing ointment, so the unguent-jar may have been a fetish or feature of her worship in pre-dynastic times. Perhaps more likely, followers of Bastet wandered into the eastern Egyptian Delta with Libyan tribes—possibly along with the domesticated cat itself—circa 3000 BCE. It is wise to note that Bastet's primitive link with the Heliopolitan solar god, Atum (or Atum-Ra), indicates that she was probably a rather warlike entity at the outset, a *uraeus* goddess personifying the relentless power and dominion of the sun, much like the closely related deity Sekhmet.

Though the Pyramid Texts depict Bastet as yet another, typical mother-figure to Pharaoh, artifacts from the time of King Hetepsekhemwy (2890 BCE) portray Bastet with the head of a lioness, fortifying the notion that her initial persona was far more pugnacious than playful. The fact that these early images of Bastet came from Saqqara, very near the Memphite cult center of Sekhmet, may indicate that the two goddesses were perhaps different dimensions of one ancestral divinity. Still, their actual relationship in those formative years remains largely unclear.

From Lioness to Domestic Cat

Toward the end of the Middle Kingdom, we notice a shift in Bastet's image and characteristics; there is a gradual decline in the lioness motif and an increasing portrayal of the goddess in the form of a smiling, domestic mother-cat. This served to downplay any lingering violence in her nature. Adding to the notion of Bastet's benevolence, she was often depicted as holding the sacred sistrum rattle, the *Utchat* Eye, or the *menat* necklace—ritual accessories of joy, magic, and appeasement likely on syncretistic loan from Bastet's *other* cultic cousin, the goddess Hathor. Keeping in mind that ancient Egyptian goddess-personalities were easily fused, it should not surprise us to understand Bastet, Sekhmet, and Hathor as ultimately interchangeable figures. To complete Bastet's popular reputation, her votive images often featured a bevy of kittens at her feet. All of these benign motifs were utilized to indicate that she was, at heart, a warm and endearing goddess, full of affection and thus representative of what we might now loosely term "family values."

The association of Bastet with the common Egyptian housecat became the most durable manifestation of this goddess and gave her an accessibility that could not readily be matched, for example, by a more ominous figure like Sekhmet. Even so, for most of the Middle Kingdom it was Sekhmet of Memphis who enjoyed regal and political clout throughout Egypt. Bastet, though well-known across the Two Lands, was largely considered to be Sekhmet's provincial cousin—wild, playfully untamed, and as mysterious as the Nile Delta region wherein she dwelled. The cheerful cat goddess, however, owned her particular territory like no other. Her first and greatest cult center was the aforementioned city of Per-

Bast or "House of Bastet." This city was the capital of Nome XVIII of Lower Egypt, situated in the eastern portion of the Delta not terribly far from the seat of the solar cult at Heliopolis.

At Per-Bast, there is evidence that Bastet was honored with a temple from at least the time of Dynasty II (almost 3000 BCE), making her one of Egypt's oldest goddesses. Her reputation must have extended beyond her namesake town even then, for the great pyramid builders Kheops and Khephren appear to have left their mark on certain artifacts and monumental remnants in Per-Bast. From an early time, the shrine of Bastet became one of the Delta's most sacred sites and various projects there were enhanced by the likes of Pharaohs Amenemhet III (1817-1772 BCE) Osorkon I (924-909 BCE) and II (883-855 BCE), and Nectanebos II (360-343 BCE) later on.

Despite the antiquity of her cult, Bastet would acquire widespread goddess-superstardom only at a relatively later epoch of Egyptian history. Her meteoric rise went hand-in-hand with the economic and political gains made by her city and its district. Thus, when Per-Bast grew ever more prosperous by securing control of various trade routes, Bastet's fame and power increased exponentially. Her popularity reached its zenith in this respect with the rise of Dynasty XXII "Libyan Pharaohs" like the Osorkon family, who abruptly shifted the royal throne from

Thebes and Tanis in 945 BCE and made the city of Per-Bast their working capital for a time.

Such political endorsement afforded enormous exposure for Bastet. With the onset of the Late Period (712-332 BCE) there was a proliferation of her images and shrines throughout Egypt. At this juncture, the maternal attributes of Isis and Hathor were incorporated into the cat-cult and soon, almost all former traces of Bastet's ferocious nature vanished. She would, however, retain her association with Sekhmet—in the sense that both goddesses could be viewed as protectresses of pregnant women and were believed to wield great powers against the forces of disease and catastrophe. Unlike Sekhmet, Bastet was sometimes said to personify the gentler, more beneficent qualities of the sun and occasionally—as the "other" Eye of Ra—the soothing rays of the moon.

This stance allowed Bastet to maintain her long-standing relationship with Atum-Ra, a conglomerate deity who had been mythically devoted to her from the beginning. At times, he appears as Bastet's father, lover, or (as one legend asserts) her savior. According to this tale, the sun god rescued the cat goddess from a devastating scorpion sting and likewise when she found herself choking on a bone! Obviously, these sorts of calamities befell many beloved Egyptian housecats and duly found their way into legend.

Bastet's association with the less-devastating attributes of the sun translated into other prerogatives, not the least of which included agriculture. The season in which the sun did not mercilessly singe the annual crop was definitely cause for celebration, and celebration never hurt the promulgation of *any* Egyptian goddess-cult.

The Goddess of Celebration

Bastet's chief reputation among the ancient Egyptians of the New Kingdom and Late Period was as a goddess of unbridled celebration. This festive characteristic had long been bolstered by links with the equally ribald rites of Hathor and Sekhmet. The annual Festival of the cat goddess at Per-Bast was, quite frankly, Egypt's most renowned drunkfest. We who are separated from the heyday of Bastet by the ages do not lack for eyewitness accounts of such hoopla. No less a historian than Herodotus "partied" with the cat goddess (and her many supplicants) in the fifth century BCE. Herodotus preserved the memory of this event in a way that betokens all the mayhem and mania of a contemporary Mardi Gras festival in Rio or New Orleans.

As Bastet's festival-day approached, the Nile River was crammed with barge after barge of pilgrims sailing to Per-Bast's most famous temple, from all parts of Egypt. These revelers grew more inebriated as their journey progressed. Drinking, carousing, and singing as they drifted, the real rites began upon arrival in the holy city, where music was played on every street, untold gallons of wine were imbibed, and the brutal life of toiling for survival along the Nile was temporarily forgotten. The wild processions to the city of Per-Bast were quite a sight for riverbank observers, since Herodotus notes that the drunken boaters would expose themselves to onlookers as the spirit moved them to do so. The great historian also remarks that some 700,000 people gathered annually for the Festival of Bastet at Per-Bast, consuming more wine during their stay than was consumed during the rest of the year throughout the entirety of Egypt.

The Cult of Bastet

For centuries, the cult of Bastet reigned supreme in her Delta hideaway. There, various male deities were subsidiary to *her* worship. Gods like Atum and Horhekenu possessed smaller temples of their own in town, but special attention was accorded to the ferocious Mihos—a deity who also owned a cult temple in the neighboring town of Leontonopolis. Though Mihos was a significant local god, he never took precedence over Bastet. Instead, he played a role as her son in the official cult. At her peak, Bastet was also honored with important cults at Heliopolis, Saqqara, Memphis, and Thebes, especially in the New Kingdom. At Thebes she rightfully took her place as part of an apparent goddess-conglomerate, along with Hathor, Sekhmet, and Mut. In the glorious Temple of Mut, Bastet was likewise venerated under the title "Mistress of Asheru," denoting the sacred lake surrounding the temple and Bastet's role as a manifestation of the chief Theban goddess.

As a goddess with such festive and esoteric qualities, Bastet was one of the few Egyptian deities with enough appeal to eventually find worship in other parts of the Mediterranean world. In Greco-Roman times, Bastet (like so many goddesses) was virtually absorbed by the figure of Isis and, as part of *that* goddess' cultic juggernaut, the cat-goddess was eventually known to the citizens of distant Rome, Ostia, Naples, and other locales. Her widespread reputation as a kind yet inherently magical deity was possibly one of the reasons that the domestic cat was later perceived to have such occult significance in Europe and elsewhere.

Ever-Beloved in Egypt

Genuine reverence for the housecat remained Bastet's most enduring asset in Egypt. Quite famous is the story of a certain Roman official that accidentally killed someone's cat while driving his chariot during a visit to Egypt. The hapless hit-and-run visitor paid for the incident at the hands of an angry mob which allegedly tore him limb from limb. The great temple at Per-Bast—known for its sleek, cat-like elegance and scope of "one hundred furlongs" on every side—was well-maintained even after the Roman occupation. The sanctuary owned vast burial grounds kept strictly for the embalmed bodies of felines. Most of these animals have been identified by forensic archaeologists as the species *felis maniculatis.* These housecats, once deceased, were mourned with great solemnity by their owners. Whole families shaved their eyebrows in sadness and, in other parts of Egypt, often sent the mummified remains of their pets to the city of Per-Bast for burial under the protective watch of Bastet.

While the role of the domestic cat in Bastet's cult was intrinsic, admirers of this deity should know that her ritual demands were not always marked by gentle affection. Perhaps as a reminder that she was once a ferocious entity demanding slaughter and sacrifice, there is evidence that some temple kittens were raised specifically to have their delicate necks throttled as offerings to their smiling, sistrum-rattling patroness. This, of course, was the work of a priesthood who believed in the necessity of such bloodshed. In general, the temple of Bastet was a sanctuary and safe-haven for hundreds of her sacred "children," who were allowed to roam freely about the premises and were treated like royalty. It is said that cats have never forgotten such treatment.

REMNANTS OF BASTET: Today's visitor is encouraged to seek out some of the exquisite statuary of Bastet—hearkening from many Egyptian periods—now preserved and showcased in the magnificent Cairo Museum. Sadly, the modern Egyptian town of "Tell-Basta" retains its goddess's ancient name but very little of her sanctuary. The site is a shambles and worth a visit only for the most intrepid wanderers indeed. Even so, archaeologists have discovered that portions of the extant edifice date from Dynasty VI (2345-2184) and were built upon a unique quasi-island in the middle of a sacred canal or lake—just as described by Herodotus. Pharaohs of the Ramesside period built here and the aforementioned Libyan Pharaohs of Dynasty XXII lavished great riches upon a temple that Herodotus also called the "most pleasing to behold in all of Egypt."

Within the present complex are the scant outlines of a smaller shrine dedicated to the feisty Mihos, and evidence of the satellite temples of Atum and Horhekenu also exists. Naturally, remnants of the famed cat-necropolis are nearby, reminding us of the time when goddesses could drive evil spirits from the land with a mere shake of the sistrum and when felines, sleek and sensual, provided mere mortals with a glimpse of the divine.

<u>Hathor</u>
Chief Role: Goddess of Love, Mirth, Music, and Vengeance
Chief Title: "The Golden One"
Cult Centers: Dendara, Aphroditopolis, Cusae, Edfu, etc.

When the ancient Egyptians chose one animal to embody everything that is beautiful, joyful, fertile, and sensual about womanhood, they opted for the cow. Lest any woman take offense at such identification, it must be realized that the need to deify a mother figure was strong in the religious sensibilities of the Nile people. After all, they tended to utilize those animals that were crucial to their lifestyles. In this case, the cow was a prime candidate for deification. She gave sustenance not only to her own offspring, but provided for the wellbeing of men and women throughout the Two Lands, often ensuring survival in a most precarious environment. When first conceptualizing the attributes of the vast Firmament above, the Egyptians and their theologians pictured the belly of a magnificent bovine.

The Antiquity of Cow-Worship

The emergence of a cow-goddess heralded one of the oldest forms of religious expression in ancient Egypt; there is evidence of bovine-orientated cults from at least 3000 BCE. To be certain, a number of far-flung deities boasted the characteristics of the cow in both the Archaic and the early Dynastic periods. For example, the Pyramid Texts make mention of Mehueret, the celestial cow that gave birth to the sky and provided the initial dwelling-place for the creator god, Atum. Mehueret's nickname was "The Great Flood" and she was considered to be the alter-ego of both Neith of Sais and Hathor of Dendera, the two chief female deities of the first Dynasties.

Nevertheless, there were other members of the "cow club." An important cult devoted to the sistrum-goddess, Bat, was centered at a very early juncture in the Upper Egyptian city of Hwt-Sekhem, later known to Greek occupationists as Diospolis Parva. Yet another goddess, Hesat, played a role as wet-nurse of Pharaoh in *his* manifestation as a golden calf. Though each of these goddesses made a contribution to the religious landscape of ancient Egypt, Hathor was either a personality derived from a combination of them all, or the one goddess with enough popularity to completely absorb and assimilate the attributes of her rivals. Whatever the scenario, Hathor rose to undisputed power at a very early stage to take her place as the greatest goddess of ancient Egypt.

The Name of Hathor

Many scholars are convinced that the goddess's ancient Egyptian name *Hwt-Hrw* means "[Temple] Enclosure of Horus," and those who disagree would be hard-pressed to find an alternative meaning. After all, the hieroglyphic sign for Hathor's name is obvious in that regard. Her designation as the "Dwelling Place" of Horus the falcon-god reinforces not only the idea that Hathor was a deity associated with the sky and the firmament (due to probable links with Mehueret and Hesat), but it also indicates how very early Hathor's identity was linked with that of Horus, who "dwelled" in the mythical Sky represented by Hathor herself, and even more tellingly in cult centers adjacent to those of the goddess. Though there can be no doubt about her ancient relationship with Horus, Hathor's cult seems far too old and powerful to have seen its goddess defined solely in terms of Horus's prerogatives. This increases the likelihood that Hathor was indeed the product of a conglomeration of many different cosmic cow-goddesses, crystallized into one identity meant—at some stage—to serve as a specific companion to Horus.

Other scholars contend that the name *Hwt-Hrw* could also have been translated as "Enclosure of the Face" because *Hr* (by itself) can, in some instances, be understood to mean "face" in very ancient Egyptian terminology. This idea is made rather attractive by the fact that the earliest known depiction of a cow-goddess occurs on the five thousand year-old Palette of King Narmer. On this palette, the face of the goddess is portrayed in full frontal fashion, a rarity throughout the history of Egyptian iconography and possibly specific to the cult of the goddess Bat of Hwt-Sekhem. If Hathor was *really* a derivative of Bat at the outset—a derivative tailored to fit specific needs and themes of the Horus cult—the translation of her name (or her sanctuary's name) as "Enclosure of the Face" may have been a serendipitous play on words interpreted to coin an ideal, alternate translation that also worked as "[Temple] Enclosure of Horus." This theory is far from certain; Hathor's Horus-name may have been strictly manufactured, with the original name of the actual goddess forever lost or her identity representative of one of the other bovine deities already mentioned.

The Rise of Hathor

Once established, Hathor's primitive cult spread quickly throughout several nomes of Upper Egypt in tandem with the cult of Horus. Dendara in Upper Egyptian Nome II and Hierakonopolis seem to have been primary launch-sites. Hathor's ascendance was unquestionably early (she officially appears as "Hathor" in Dynasty IV—2575-2467 BCE) and in every place she was inexorably linked with Horus as the typical yet highly functional combination of mother, wet-nurse, and consort. She was also one of the few ancient Egyptian goddesses to have had her own retinue of female "prophets" (or *hm-netjer* priests) in addition to the ubiquitous male cult personnel.

As a mythical and popular figure, Hathor was not merely an adjunct of Horus. On the contrary, she was marvelously flexible and came to assume various functions with amazing ease. By Dynasty V (2465-2345 BCE) and the composition of the Pyramid Texts, Mehueret, Hathor, Hesat, and even the Heliopolitan goddess Nut are listed as personifications of the Firmament—mammoth cows with bodies spread from one end of the horizon to the other, their bellies emblazoned with stars. But the realms of music, beauty, sex, femininity, and wild celebration belonged most specifically to Hathor above all others, as we shall see.

Throughout her illustrious history, Hathor would never relinquish all of her bovine attributes, indicating that it was she who set the strongest cow-standard from the earliest days. Accordingly, she was variously portrayed in complete cow form, as a woman with a cow's ears and horns, or as a woman distinguished by a headdress of cow's horns surrounding the solar disc. This was her most famous and maternal image, one that denoted her equally close association with the god Ra, especially in his Horus or "Horakhty" manifestation.

From the time of Dynasty V, the Heliopolitan theologians recognized Hathor's already astonishing importance as a national goddess. Although they did not include her in the Great Ennead of Heliopolis, they certainly gave her choice cameo roles in their convoluted tales of creation, as well as an important cult in their magnificent city. Quite apart from the Ennead, which had its own distinct cosmological and familial concerns, Hathor was viewed as a thoroughly independent divinity. She was the favored daughter of Ra himself and sometimes also his mother and his consort, just as she had been both mother and consort to Horus. The personalities of Ra and Hathor were perceived as being so intimate that one variant of myth tells of the goddess performing a striptease for her "father" simply as a means of cheering him up during a depressive episode.

Hathor's powerful presence in Heliopolis and also at Memphis allowed her to assimilate the aspects of two important lioness-goddesses: Tefnut and Sekhmet. Thus she acquired one of her most distinctive personalities, the ferocious, out-of-control force that sought vengeance upon the enemies of Pharaoh and of Ra. In this form, Hathor became the avenging *uraeus* or "Eye of Ra" *par excellence,* a completely transmogrified entity. In the persona of a raging lioness she was the Slaughterer—the "Distant" or "Wandering" goddess, who prowled the deserts and frontiers of Egypt as a malevolent destroyer of life. Only through appeasement with the sistrum rattle and various other temple rites could the lioness be coaxed figuratively back from the outskirts and restored to her mirthful aspect.

It is in this guise that Hathor represented for the Egyptians the chaotic and oppressive forces of nature that were automatically associated with the hardships of life along the Nile valley. Only when placated and transformed into her joyful "cow-self" could the goddess of drunken revelry take her place at the very heart of an agriculturally functional Egypt.

Again, the myth in which Hathor figures prominently as the raging Eye of Ra was not so much about revenge, but rather linked with the flood cycles upon which the Egyptians staked their very lives. Without question, the sun (at its worst) could bring widespread death and destruction when accompanied by drought. Hathor's persona was bound up with this annual tension, this drama. At the height of summer, her fury would blaze across Egypt in the form of the murderous solar disc, the "Eye moving toward Nubia" as the season began to diminish. The fruitful flood that followed was a sure sign of Eye-Goddess pacification. The diminishing power of the sun and the abundance of the inundation proved a restorative and soothing relief to the land. Hathor's greatness rested in the fact that she could embody such polarized aspects, and this early capacity for duality helped make her the most powerful goddess in the minds and hearts of the ancient Egyptian people. As a national goddess she was much more important than Isis, for example, for the greater part of Egyptian history. She was enormously popular even after Isis later usurped her dominance.

The Hathorian myth in which the natural dichotomy of feast-or-famine was couched is amusing and familiar enough to many cultures; it has some sort of variant in almost every mythological cycle of the ancient world. In this particular story, a terribly insecure Ra gazes upon the earth to see that humanity has not lived up to his expectations. Even the other gods begin to make fun of him, declaring that his shrines are neglected and empty. As a balm for his wounded psyche, Hathor takes the form of Ra's raging Eye and embarks upon a murderous campaign across Egypt. She is ordered to kill every man, woman, and child she encounters in her devastating form as a lioness. She essentially *becomes* that "other" Eye and Daughter of Ra: Sekhmet the Terrible.

As the marauding Hathor goes about her business, she becomes increasingly drunk on human blood and Ra realizes that there will be no one left to worship him at all if she kills the entire populace. He repents his anger against humanity, but there is a catch: Hathor, once turned loose, is not so easily reined-in. Ra is forced to play a ruse on Hathor in order to stop the goddess in her tracks. Brewing great pots of beer—a staple of Hathor's wild temple festivals—Ra uses red ochre from the First Cataract region of the Nile to dye the beverage and "fool" Hathor into believing the stuff was human blood.

The goddess paused in her onslaught and drank heavily, becoming so inebriated that she quickly abandoned her ferocious mindset and gave in to revelry. For this reason, beer was of great importance to cultic rites centered upon Hathor and crucial to the everyday people that celebrated her annual return to "good spirits." In fact, an inscription on the walls of her massive temple in Dendera purports to give the exact brewing recipe Ra used to calm the goddess down.

The Joyful Hathor

As noted in the case of the cat-goddess of Per-Bast, the ancient Egyptians welcomed almost any excuse to feast and make merry. They deserved it; life was hard along the Nile. The fact that such revelry was sanctioned by a loaded religious calendar made celebration a frequent occurrence. Numerous festivals were held in honor of Hathor throughout Egypt, almost all of them notorious for consuming entire towns and cities in a flood of orgiastic glee. Thus, the Mother-Consort of Horus and Daughter of Ra solidified her position as ideal patroness of any art associated with happiness—from beer and wine-making to the musical arts.

Dendara in Upper Egypt remained the chief center of Hathor's worship. Here, as elsewhere, she was closely associated with the all-pervasive worship of Horus. Of course, this relationship gave Hathor an extremely important role in official Pharaonic cult. Since Pharaoh, while living, was "one with Horus," Hathor was *de facto* his mother, wife, nurse, and lover. In this manner, her influence extended to the Egyptian throne from a very early date, in which context she was considered the Great Golden Cow providing nourishment for the child-King, empowering him for the benefit of Egypt. The Queen (or a pharaoh's favorite wife) was often equated with Hathor. Beauty remained the domain of Hathor, who was said to exceed all other goddesses in physical appeal. Perhaps no Queen better exemplified this identification than Nefertari, the "Beautiful Companion" of Ramses II, who appears in the guise of Hathor at the little temple of Abu Simbel.

Though, as mentioned, many assume that Isis was always the most important goddess in the Egyptian pantheon, it was really Hathor who wielded the most influence, at least until the Late Period, when the beloved Isis began her rise to a more nationalistic form of supremacy. The prior preeminence of Hathor was mainly due to her proximity to the royal house and also to the enormous power accrued and wielded by her priesthood in so many temples across Egypt. Like Isis, Hathor's status was further enhanced by the fact that she could play a great funerary role in ancient religious thought.

Mistress of the West

At Thebes and elsewhere, Hathor showed her versatility not only as milk-provider and guardian of the living king, but as "Mistress of the West"—fearsome protectress of the Theban necropolis, or burial grounds. The arid hills and canyons that loomed in the Valleys of the Kings and Queens were considered Hathor's unique territory, for the desolate quality of the region captured the dualism in Hathor's personality in most exquisite fashion. In the "West," the place that "opened up the way" to Duat, the Underworld, Hathor was seen as a mighty friend of the deceased and even as an attendant of the shadowy Lord of the Underworld, Osiris. Her most compelling image in this setting was that of a great cow emerging from the Land of the Dead to browse among the papyrus plants, which were also sacred to her. Her role as a mortuary goddess was so distinct that it became manifest in a completely unique deity—Amentet or Hathor-Amentet. Her image is found throughout the lonely tombs to this very day.

Hathor the National Goddess

Beyond Thebes and Dendara, Hathor was worshiped in just about every Egyptian community of note. Though Isis did eclipse (or absorb) Hathor's widespread popularity among the common people, no goddess in ancient Egypt owned more temples or sanctuaries. At Memphis, her vengeful side was highly regarded as a manifestation of Sekhmet and she owned a strategically located temple there as the proprietress of a sacred Sycamore Tree. As "Mistress of the Sycamore," Hathor was said to stand among the boughs and pour nourishment into the mouths of the newly deceased. An entire cult centered upon this holy tree in Memphis and even the living gathered to partake of its spiritual benefits just as the dead were supposed to do in the afterlife. In this manner, Hathor was equated with the Firmament Goddess, Nut, and both were thus interchangeable as healing goddesses of Memphis.

Healing powers were not lacking in Hathor's cult center at Dendara, either. The ancients considered her temple there to be the source of curative powers emanating from the goddess. From at least Ptolemaic times, a portion of her outlying temple complex was reserved as a *sanatorium* for those seeking miraculous cures. According to archaeologists, water was first poured over a sacred image of the goddess and was then either consumed by the supplicant or irrigated into special "bathing areas" for purposes of bodily immersion (think Lourdes, France, but with a different "Lady" in charge). Hopefuls were then given various herbs to induce a trance-like state and thereafter taken to individual "cells" wherein it was hoped that Hathor herself would "visit" to enact the needed cure. Such faith in Hathor's healing powers may have stemmed from or inspired a popular scene in some versions of the Horus mythological cycle. According to such tales, it was Hathor who poured gazelle's milk into the gouged eye-sockets of Horus after he was attacked by Set. Her spell healed the all-important sight of Horus (signified by the "restored" Udjat Eye) and enabled the god to continue his battle for the throne of Egypt (see the entry about *Isis*).

Goddess of the Outskirts

Even on the very frontiers of the ancient Egyptian empire, Hathor held unique sway. In the mining settlement of Serabit El-Khadim on the Sinai Peninsula, she played a significant role as "Mistress of Turquoise" from the Old Kingdom until at least the time of Ramses VII (1279-1213 BCE). In that outlying region, precious turquoise and copper were mined under the patronage of Hathor. The ruins of her lonesome, rambling temple are still extant there. In most places, Hathor was regarded as the goddess who oversaw the mining of gold, a role reflected in her association with the brilliant solar disc and in one of her most popular titles, "The Golden One."

Mistress of the Temple of Horus

Next to that of Osiris and Isis, the marriage of Hathor and Horus was likely the most revered partnership in the Egyptian pantheon. This alliance was also the object of one of the kingdom's greatest festivals. With the coming of the New Moon in what we now call May, the priests of Hathor's temple at Dendara lavished her sacred image in stunning attire. Placing it on her sacred barge in the Nile, these priests sent Hathor on an annual cruise to Horus' temple at Edfu, over one hundred kilometers distant. Thousands of pilgrims flocked the riverbanks to ogle as the holy bark made its lazy way, the entire event being the cause of widespread celebration. Along the journey, Hathor's bark made various stops so that her sacred image could hobnob with other goddesses and gods. Ancient texts tell us that her itinerary included a stop to "visit" Mut in the Temple at Asheru in Thebes, Nekhbet in El-Kab, and even Anukis and Nephthys at their temple in Komir.

Once in Edfu, the real festival began. Horus (in statue form) "greeted" Hathor in his own bark at the city dock and, with much fanfare, priests would trundle the two lovers into a private, specially appointed love-sanctuary where the two images could spend the night getting reacquainted. The people of Edfu would dance, drink, and make merry as priests and priestesses shook their *menat* necklaces and rattled their *sistra.*

This "Festival of Beautiful Meeting" at Edfu was one of the most ribald and well-attended of the Egyptian holidays, almost on a par with Bastet's party in the north. It was noted for its free food and drink—all supplied by the powerful temple estates of Hathor and Horus. None of the faithful seemed to care that, after fourteen days, the two deities went back to dwelling in their separate residences. In truth, Hathor owned a permanent and prestigious cult-chamber in the temple at Edfu and received worship there year-round, just as Horus was honored at Dendara.

The Motherly Goddess

Since a mother-goddess isn't worth much without children, Hathor was associated with at least two offspring via the partnership with Horus. Ihy, a child-god of music and general gaiety, was venerated in conjunction with his mother at Dendara and a second child, Harsomtus, was a Horus-clone thought to personify the union of the Two Lands wrought by his esteemed father. Throughout the history of her cult, the perception of Hathor as a friend to mothers and newborns was as strong as any other aspect of her career. This is well-attested by the popularity of the Seven Hathors—a group of "fairy godmother-ish" goddesses who made themselves available at the moment of birth to ensure good health and predict a positive destiny for the offspring.

With each passing century in ancient Egyptian history, Hathor's influence remained strong, losing no momentum in Ptolemaic and Roman times despite the ascension of Isis. The rulers of those periods honored her with the magnificently rebuilt sanctuary still standing at Dendara and numerous other temples and renovations throughout the land. Cities like Aphroditopolis, Cusae, Imaou, Kom Ombo, Heliopolis, and Memphis continued to be strongholds of the worship of the Golden One. Alongside Isis, she remained the most beloved goddess of the people, even though the last centuries of Egyptian religion saw these two deities become increasingly fused, with Isis emerging as the dominant personality. Indeed, it must be remembered that, even though Hathor appears to have been the possible original "mother of Horus," she generally relinquished her overtly maternal prerogatives once the Osiris-Isis cult rose to supremacy in the hearts and imaginations of the ancient Egyptians. In all places and periods, Hathor was celebrated for her own, independent qualities and as the ideal mate for Horus—making her perhaps the most distinctly pharaonic goddess in the vast Egyptian pantheon.

REMNANTS OF HATHOR: Hathor is everywhere amid the extant monuments and artifacts of ancient Egypt, from Cairo to Abu Simbel. Even so, her breathtaking temple-complex at Dendara must be seen to be believed. If your Egyptian itinerary does not include a stop at Dendara, it is more than worth a well-planned side-trip. Always ask a reliable guide; the site has often been closed due to archaeological or political factors.

Heqet

Chief Role: Goddess of Fertility and Childbirth
Chief Title: "Mistress of Har-Wer"
Cult Centers: Antinoopolis, Qus

Though Heqet was almost always depicted in the form of (or with the face of) the seemingly lowly frog, she, too, was one of the more popular and important goddesses in the Egyptian pantheon. Though her actual origins are as murky as a swamp, her place in birthing-tradition and folklore was very distinct. Some have postulated that Heqet originated as part of the Ogdoad of Hermopolis, as the female portion of the Huh/Huhet duo. However, it should be remembered that only the male deities of the Ogdoad boasted amphibian heads; the females bore serpentine faces. Heqet was undeniably a *goddess*—sensual, fertile, and always linked with the travails of birth and other regenerative aspects of the human experience.

Honoring a frog-goddess came naturally to the ancient Egyptians, who were apparently quite impressed by the way frogs proliferated in the millions during the flood season. In this sense, the frog was an obvious sign of fertility. Though the motif of the frog was already known from the male gods of the Ogdoad, Heqet emerged at an early date as a goddess with her own cult and identity. From the time of the Pyramid Texts, she appears as yet another patroness of Pharaoh's body during his dangerous ascension toward the Firmament after death.

It has been suggested that Heqet was actually the most important of the various Nile inundation-gods, at the outset. Her amphibious nature notwithstanding, any primacy she possessed in this regard was later usurped by powerful *male* deities like Khnum and Hapy. If Heqet were indeed the patroness of the inundation at the beginning, her later cultic association with Khnum would be easily understandable. In this scenario, the male deity absorbed her attributes but delegated for Heqet a role pertaining to the more feminine aspects of fecundity and generation.

Fecundity was Heqet's *oeuvre*. The life-cycle of the frog was so reliable along the banks of the Nile during a good flood that Egyptian women could easily recognize the value of a goddess who might, by association, ensure their own reproductive powers and a healthy existence for their offspring. Thus, as ram-headed Khnum spun worlds into being on his potter's wheel, Heqet was the companion deity who instilled the life-force *(ankh)* into all that Khnum fashioned—including babies. This is why she is often depicted in temple reliefs on her knees before Khnum and his manufactured humans, gently pressing the *ankh* to their lips and investing them with the breath of life.

Perhaps the most famous of these representations is found on the walls of the Temple of Hatshepsut at Deir el-Bahri, where Heqet is shown in the presence of her other collaborators in childbirth, Bes and Taweret. Ancient Egyptian women also fashioned frog amulets to secure fertility and successful birth. Such skills even allowed Heqet to score a cameo role in the Osirian melodrama; there, she was sometimes part of the cluster of deities helping Isis resurrect her murdered husband. For this reason, Heqet was an important part of Osirian rites that took place at the holy city of Abydos. For this reason (and perhaps due to localized tradition), a cult statue of Heqet was in residence at Abydos, tended by her own retinue of priests; a shrine seems to have been installed by Seti I himself.

Despite constant prestige, Heqet's association with Khnum was overshadowed in the New Kingdom by Satis and Anukis. These ladies of the First Cataract region eventually became the primary associates of the ram-headed deity. She found a solid companion, however, in the god Haroeris. At ancient Har-Wer (Qus), a Greco-Roman temple was jointly dedicated to them and its scant ruins still stand today. Elsewhere, Heqet was worshiped at appropriately soggy locales. Antinoopolis (drowning-site site of Antinous, the Roman emperor Hadrian's lover) was famous for its temple of Heqet and she was likewise venerated in parts the Fayyum oasis region.

Despite powerful links with the inundation, flood-control skills were seemingly not *always* part of the goddess' magical repertoire; an inscription from the famed Tomb of Petosiris depicts Heqet pleading for one of her washed-out sanctuaries to be rebuilt and fortified against future catastrophe!

REMNANTS OF HEQET: Heqet is a bit more difficult to find amid the ruins of ancient Egypt, compared to other goddesses. The paltry remains of her temple at Qus are not really worth a visit, but depending upon the state of archaeological affairs at any given time, one can view the classic birth-scene featuring Heqet at Hatshepsut's temple at Deir el-Bahri. Also, be certain to wander into the *mammisi* (or "divine birth-house") at Philae; Heqet the frog-headed is prominent in this peripteral temple's iconography.

Isis

Chief Role: Goddess of Magic and Motherhood
Chief Title: "Lady Great of Magic"
Cult Centers: Philae, Behbeit, Alexandria, etc.

Hardly enough can be said about the greatness of the Egyptian goddess Isis. Not only did she become the most personally beloved and respected of all the immortals of the Two Lands, she went on to become (arguably) the most widely worshipped pagan deity in the ancient world. Her cult began over 5000 years ago, likely in a backwater of the Nile Delta and, believe it or not, Isis is still worshipped today by any number of Egyptian "restorationists." It can perhaps be said that only the Virgin Mary has made a more formidable *feminine* impact on the spiritual life of Western civilization as we now know it.

In the ancient Egyptian religious hierarchy, Osiris and Horus were the more officially important divinities, with Isis (like most goddesses) acting as mere adjunct, but it was Isis whose popularity came to transcend that of both her husband and offspring—Isis who became the point of reference by which her own family members and most of the other Egyptian deities were eventually defined and regarded.

Goddess of the Delta?

It is more than a trifle uncertain where Isis first appeared on the Egyptian religious horizon. Some believe she originated in the Nile Delta region, perhaps near the modern site of Behbeit el-Hagar. By Ptolemaic times, this town and its enormous temple were dedicated to Isis in her guise as the "The Festive Goddess"—basically a mistress of ceremonies in rites that enabled her murdered husband, Osiris, to rise again annually and bring abundance to the kingdom. In pre-dynastic times, it is possible that Isis was a local fertility goddess in this vicinity. The fact that she was so early paired with Osiris, who may have been the native god of the neighboring town of Djedu (Busiris), lends added plausibility to the notion that "Per-

Hebitet" ("Domain of the Festive Goddess") was her place of origin. However, Isis does not even occur in the extant records until the composition of the Dynasty V Pyramid Texts. There only is she first associated with Osiris, and allusions to the water-pots of a certain "Hebitet" in the Pyramid Texts are as inconclusive as any idea that the goddess actually originated in this district.

This being noted, any pre-dynastic qualities of Isis were likely centered upon the typical fertility/motherhood motifs common to virtually all Egyptian goddesses. The "throne-like" hieroglyphic sign for her name (worn atop her head or crown in many cases) may not give us as much information about her beginnings as some contend.

While this glyph eventually pertained to the royal throne and would indeed come to have pharaonic connotations in her later career, it is problematic to consider Isis a personification of the Egyptian throne at the outset. Such positions were reserved for goddesses who were initially much more influential, like Hathor or Neith. Thus, the "seat" glyph could well have been a modified form of a more primitive fetish/symbol associated with the nascent cult of Isis. Another fetish in the Isis cult was the *tat.* Some researchers believe that this knot-like sign depicted the uterus, vagina, and corresponding ligaments—an interpretation that would guarantee a place for Isis as an early goddess of motherhood and sexuality.

To be certain, the cult of Isis did not make much of an impression in the early dynasties. Rather, her "marriage" to Osiris provided a stepping-stone to fame in Lower Egypt. Beginning with Dynasty V (2465-2345 BCE) both deities appear throughout the Pyramid Texts as members of the Great Ennead of Heliopolis, indicating that they had achieved at least some considerable measure of renown before the composition of the texts themselves. Within the framework of the Ennead, Isis was the first daughter born to Geb (the Earth) and Nut (the Firmament) on the fourth intercalary (or epagomenal) day. Very early in the budding Heliopolitan cosmology, we learn that Isis was a typically male-dependent Egyptian goddess. Once the mythological cycle accelerated, however, she proved to be a most durable and pro-active deity. The great things she accomplished for Osiris—and thus for Egypt—would eventually endear her to the hearts of the ancient people in extraordinary ways.

The Legends of Isis

Starting with the basic Heliopolitan cosmology of the Pyrmaid Texts, Isis-mythology developed along complex lines that merged, overlapped, and even borrowed from other cultures and influences over the long centuries of Egyptian religious tradition. By the time Plutarch captured his version of the legend(s) in the late first century CE, they had been compromised by mistakes in Plutarch's interpretation and by any number of interpolations that may or may not have derived from the evolution of actual Egyptian thought.

Even so, there are many motifs and themes in Plutarch's account which can be viably traced back to the most archaic traditions about Isis and her associated deities. Since any fixed mythical tradition is essentially an accumulation of lore from a variety of sources, it behooves us to first examine the general, most well-known versions and fragments. Thereafter we can ponder which elements of the myth may be genuinely Egyptian and which may be accretions. In any event, because we are dealing with myth, it is not possible to dismiss any feature, out of hand, as being spurious. Every aspect of a successful myth is essentially an addition deemed necessary to the evolution of that particular legend in order to suit the immediate needs of audiences *over time*; the goal of the researcher should be to examine the probable nature and purpose of such developments.

Beginning with the Pyramid Texts, we learn that Isis was the first daughter born to Geb and Nut, and was said to have married her brother, Osiris, just as her other siblings, Set and Nephthys, became partners. In this fashion, all of the children of Geb and Nut appear to have lived in a dualistic "earthly dimension" among the hierarchy of Heliopolitan gods. While each one of them was invested with enormous magical power and influence, they were believed by the Egyptians to have occupied a more distinctly *human* realm of existence than their cosmic forbears.

Various sources tell us that, being the firstborn son of Geb and Nut, Osiris was the rightful heir to his father's hallowed throne. Once upon this throne, Osiris ruled with an unprecedented kindness and wisdom. He taught the savage tribes of the remote regions how to civilize themselves, weaning them from every manner of vice and instructing them about the cultivation of corn, barley, and other staple crops. He taught them how to establish towns and local governments and, most importantly, how to build proper temples for the gods.

During all of this positive activity, Isis was not locked away in a distant palace. Rather, she took an important role in her husband's affairs and set out on her own mission to educate the people of Egypt. She taught women the crucial arts of weaving, spinning, grinding corn-meal into flour, and various medicinal procedures required for survival. She also championed the virtues of "marriage" (committed male-female companionship) in Egyptian society and endowed women with skills in midwifery, securing for them a vital place in the home and in the community.

Most important of all, Isis took it upon herself to become a great sorceress, learning her potent craft from none other than the wise god, Thoth. An extraordinary student, Isis soon became more adept at wielding spells than her teacher, as is often the case with mythical sorcerers. It is for this reason that she became known as the goodly "Sorceress-Queen" of Egypt and it's likely the reason Osiris felt quite comfortable allowing Isis to handle affairs of state while he was absent from the capital on his own campaigns. Allowing a female figure to rule was unprecedented, but Isis proved to be as competent a monarch as her husband, according to myth.

Of course, someone's always got to ruin a good thing. This entire scenario bothered their brother, Set, to the point of distraction. Set's heart was embittered enough as it was because Osiris was given the throne of Geb. The sight of a *woman* sitting in majesty—if only in the king's absence—made him livid. One version of the myth claims that Set had his chance to rule at least the Southern realm of Egypt (no doubt a nod to his actual cultic presence there at Ombos, or Naqada) but his maniacal demands for complete control nixed the original arrangement. Another strain of legend indicates that Set was actually a co-regent with Osiris, but proved so inept at the task that their father, Geb, dethroned him.

The Betrayal of Osiris

At this point in the tale, Set began to hold clandestine meetings in which he plotted the downfall of his brother. While keeping watch over the throne, Isis became aware of these machinations and was able to thwart such plans by virtue of her magical powers. Even the mighty Isis, however, was unable to foresee the unspeakable scheme her brother was about to put into action.

Fashioning a sarcophagus (or coffin) to fit the exact dimensions of his brother's body, Set invited Osiris to a celebratory banquet as the great king passed through the city of Memphis one evening. Placing the coffin in the midst of the rowdy gathering, it was soon coveted by one and all due to such exquisite craftsmanship (and the fact that the ancient Egyptians were mad about having nice coffins). As a party-game, Set announced that he would give the chest as a gift to whoever could fit perfectly within. In their spirit of revelry, many tried but found their bodies unsuitable. Finally, the good-natured Osiris took his turn and, once snug in the coffin, Set sprung into action. A host of devious henchmen sprung forward at their master's signal and snapped-shut the lid of the coffin. Trapped, Osiris was whisked away before anyone could stop them. At the riverbank, the minions of Set sealed the coffin and cast it adrift into the Nile.

The news of this treachery spread like wildfire throughout Egypt. Upon reaching the ears of Isis (who was said to be on her own expedition in the city of Koptos), the story sent her into a tailspin of horror. Chopping off a portion of her hair in anguish, she could think only of hunting down the chest and recovering the body of her murdered beloved. Leaving the palace and the throne behind—for they were no longer hers to guard—she set out in a state of immense grief.

Her search was arduous.

First, a group of children in the Nile delta region informed Isis that the death-chest had floated all the way into the turbulent waters of the Mediterranean Sea, allegedly making landfall in distant Phoenicia. There, Isis discovered that matters had taken a turn for the worse; a particularly fast-growing tree had engulfed the chest on a beach and had grown-up *around* the coffin, concealing it from view. The king of Byblos had passed by the tree one day and decided to chop it down for use as a column in his palace. Distraught but undaunted, Isis sailed all the way to Phoenicia in her little papyrus boat, only to discover that her husband had indeed been turned into a piece of royal palace décor. Resourceful goddess that she was, Isis concocted a plan to infiltrate the king's palace and recover her husband's body.

Using her sorcery, Isis transformed her appearance into that of a lowly nursemaid and acquired a job at the palace, tending the infant son of the queen—played in one strain of myth by the great Phoenician goddess, Astarte, in a rather memorable cameo role. An enchanted perfume was the agent of deception in this account, for it is said that the scent of Isis so bewitched everyone in the palace that she was given unlimited access to the young Prince of Byblos. This portion of the myth, one might add, is clearly an attempt to incorporate elements of the Greek legend of Demeter and Persephone.

Isis—Griller of Phoenician Babies

While in charge of the prince, Isis began to take a certain pity upon the boy in his frailty. She decided to render a favor by using her powers to endow the infant with a measure of immortality. A simple spell was required, one in which Isis gave the boy her thumb to suck upon instead of her breast. There was also another, incidental detail: the child had to be placed in the midst of a blazing fire in order to expunge all mortal impurities. Things went smoothly until Queen Astarte barged into the royal nursery one evening and saw her child being grilled. Clearly not familiar with this goddess "technique," she screamed.

Naturally, the spell was broken and Isis did what she should have done in the first place: she cast-off the nursemaid outfit and revealed herself in the full thrall of her power, demanding to have the column that had been cut down by the king, or *else.* Wisely, Astarte persuaded her husband to give Isis the pillar in question, and this was cut open for her at once, revealing the doomed coffin that had floated all the way from Egypt.

The Anguish of Isis

Too heartbroken to open the chest in front of strangers, Isis set sail for Egypt on a ship provided by the remorseful Phoenician ruler. Once at sea, she opened the coffin and proceeded to wail so frightfully over the corpse of Osiris that at least one young crew member dropped dead on the spot. In one variant of this story, an inquisitive child comes too close and Isis glares at him in anger until he keels—truly a "look" that could kill.

Upon reaching Egypt, Isis knew that Set had usurped the throne as its rightful heir, seeing as Osiris had not engendered a male child for the purpose of succession. Fearful that Set would use his newfound power to persecute her, Isis sequestered herself and her husband's body in the mysterious Delta swamplands. There she hid, stricken with poverty and deep in mourning while she plotted some measure of revenge against the wicked Set. She was not alone in her sadness: her shadowy but faithful sister, Nephthys, rejected the evil ways of her husband (Set) and left him to join Isis in misery. The two goddesses became partners in mourning and guarding the dead Osiris and, to keep their distinctive moans from being recognized by Set or his minions, they transformed themselves into kite-birds, swooping among the treetops to sing their anguished notes.

The Dismemberment of Osiris

According to both early and late versions of the myth, Isis and Nephthys left the body of Osiris, ostensibly to search for food. During one of their forays, the wily Set happened to discover the corpse of Osiris while on a hunting expedition of his own. Infuriated at the sight of his brother's corpse, he flew into a rage and ripped it into fourteen pieces. His powerful arm cast these pieces across the length and breadth of Egypt.

When Isis and Nephthys learned of this latest sacrilege, their grief was more intense than ever. This time, their wails brought a number of concerned gods to their side: Wadjet the cobra-goddess of Buto; Neith of Sais; and others. Combining their formidable powers, Isis and her sister set sail to search for the scattered pieces of their Beloved Osiris. The search was painstaking but ultimately successful. Wherever Isis found one of the holy appendages, she mourned it with great publicity to make Set *think* that she was finally resigned to her spouse's demise. In fact, some of the legends tell that she contrived all sorts of phony burials throughout Egypt, hoping to add to Set's potential confusion.

These many pieces of Osiris's body were given their own funerals; this is supposed to be the "reason" why so many cities in Egypt later claimed to be the repositories of precious Osirian relics. In the myth, however, Isis never buried the real pieces of Osiris. Rather, she fashioned exact *replicas* and buried those. Eventually, the Two Sisters collected every piece except the penis of the god, which Set had tossed into the Nile near Oxyrhynchus, a city that was conveniently one of Set's actual cult centers. A species of Nile fish called the Mormyrus ate the penis and was forever despised by most of the Egyptian people.

The Resurrection of Osiris

Isis and Nephthys scuttled back to the safety of the Delta with their gory collection and, after carefully putting the body back together as best they could, the sisters worked the greatest of enchantments. Under the direction of the ibis-headed god, Thoth, and aided by the ministrations of dog-headed Anubis, Isis and Nephthys performed the magical rites of embalming and mummification for the very first time. Taking once more the form of kites, the sisters fanned their goddess-wings above the body of Osiris, filling his dead lungs with the breath of immortal life.

So it was that Osiris returned to the realm of the living and the long-suffering Isis was able to gaze at last into the eyes of her beloved. The ecstasy was short-lived, however, for there was a catch to the spell—Osiris would survive, but his resurrected form was only fit for the murky underworld of the afterlife known as Duat. Only in Duat could Osiris take his throne as supreme Lord and Judge of all the dead. Realizing that she would lose the mortal reality of her husband forever, Isis fashioned a new member for him and used magic to conceive his child before he slipped away forever into the next world. This conception marked the next phase of Isis's amazing mythical adventures.

Stalwart Mother of Horus

Faced with the prospect of motherhood while in exile, Isis was forced to bring forth Horus-the-Child in the impoverished conditions of the delta swamps. Once again, other deities came to her assistance. Auntie Nephthys was given the task of fostering the child as wet-nurse, along with goddesses like Mut and Hathor. Wadjet the Cobra made her services available, as did an assortment of vagabond scorpions under the power of the goddess Serqet. All of these deities kept watchful eyes upon Horus while Isis begged for food in the nearby townships. Why her magical powers were ineffectual in the grocery-conjuring department has always been a bit of a paradox.

Unfortunately, while Isis was away on some excursion, Horus was at play with his foster-mother, Nephthys. The devious Set had transformed himself into a scorpion and with great stealth stung the child in Nephthys' very lap. Isis returned to find the child near death from the poison and, once again, her powers seem to have failed her, for she had no means by which the poison might be extracted. Nephthys was overcome with grief and her cries rang out through the marshlands until Serqet heard the commotion. When the scorpion goddess asked what had come to pass, Nephthys revealed that Horus had been attacked. Serqet, queen of scorpions, assured the goddess that none of *her* minions had committed such a foul deed and all agreed that the perpetrator had been Set himself.

At the moment of crisis, Nephthys had the good sense to recommend that Isis make an appeal to Ra, who was cruising the cosmos in his "Bark of Millions of Years." Thoth himself heard the goddesses cry out for assistance and, from his station on the Bark of Ra, descended to perform the necessary healing magic upon Horus. The sun literally stopped in its tracks to save Horus, according to the myth. Once the child was cured, Isis was more determined than ever to see her son grow up with the skills necessary to oust his vile uncle. Her plan would not come to fruition for many years, but her preparations would prove to be impeccable.

"Isis Who Knows Ra by His Secret Name"

To prepare for her coup, Isis knew that her magical powers would have to be stronger than ever. There could be no spell beyond her comprehension, no aspect of the primordial forces beyond her control. The only way to attain the auxiliary power she needed was to *grasp* that power from its ultimate source—Ra himself. Some versions of the myth imply that Isis decided to trick Ra because she was finally sick and tired of living a dual existence in the world of mortals and longed to join the great celestial company once and for all. Whatever her mythical motivation, Isis and her plan were undeniably cunning.

According to the legend, Ra was elderly and on the verge of senility, but still invulnerable to attack from any of the gods, so great was his power. Since he had created (in his form of Ra-Atum) every known being in the universe and because these beings—the good and the evil—had originated according to his will, Ra remained Master of All. Even so, Isis devised a crafty way to get around this obstacle.

Waiting in secret while Ra made his daily journey across the land of Egypt, Isis watched for the spittle that inevitably fell from the god's withered old mouth. This fluid fell upon the desert sand and Isis gathered it up after the god had passed. Working her crafty magic, Isis fashioned a venomous serpent from the mixture of sand and Ra's saliva. Then she placed this creature upon Ra's usual, daily pathway and waited in secret. The next day, as Ra made his trek, he was bitten. The ancient god screamed and writhed in pain. The resulting sound of his agony brought all of the other gods to his side, for the solar bark itself had halted in the sky with the incapacitation of its captain. The matter was truly a cosmic catastrophe:

"Let all my children assemble together—the gods to whom I gave in confidence the words of eternal power—that they may discover my enemy, who has secretly attacked my heel. Let them hold the poison at bay or I shall perish...and all of them with me!"

Upon seeing great Ra in agony, each deity offered assistance but was powerless to extract the poison. They wondered how the supreme god could have suffered such a terrible blow, but Isis alone knew why the serpent had been so successful: it was a creature made from the very substance of Ra, but *not* by his will or design. As the other gods fretted over how the universe would maintain its balance, Isis moved calmly into their midst:

Isis spoke gently to Ra, the great god, saying, "What ails you, Father? What evil of no man's doing has smitten you to your core? I pity you, but I do not worship you. I neither believe in you nor do I fear you. Perhaps because of this, great Ra, I may be better equipped to assist you. Tell me: is it a serpent that has wounded your heel? Certainly, no good thing can do evil. Certainly nothing you created has lifted up its head against you in reckless fashion?"

As Ra complained loudly of his pains and the fate of all the gods (should he perish), Isis coyly assured him that *she* could succeed where the others had failed. She promised that her spells would bring healing, but at a dear price. She would rescue Ra only if he told her his Secret Name.

Of course, this only added to Ra's agony. For the ancient Egyptians, the personal name possessed a particularly magical significance. The fact that Ra kept his true name a secret indicated that, for him, like all the gods, it contained the very essence of his power. Revealing the Name to Isis would be tantamount to making her his equal in magical potency. Therefore, Ra obfuscated admirably, tossing out several decoy names in the hope that one of *those* would satisfy the curiosity of the wily goddess:

"I am Ra, the intolerable splendor in the hot noonday! I am Atum who flourishes in glory at the break of evening!"

Isis had little interest in such evasive maneuvers. Using her magic to actually intensify the suffering of the aged god, she reminded Ra that time was running out—the poison would destroy him if he did not reveal his secret name. Finally, out of sheer pain and desperation, Ra gave in and whispered his secret into the ear (and knowledge) of Isis, making her at last his very equal in magic. Being as merciful as she was crafty, the goddess lifted the spell at once and Ra went on his solar way, grumbling at the machinations of such a tricky goddess.

These cleverly composed strains of myth were to become the most popular in ancient Egypt, capturing what the people came to love best about Isis—her cunning, her mercy, her sheer power over magical forces, and most of all, her loyalty to Osiris and the child Horus. After all, the myth reveals that Ra allowed Isis to share the knowledge of his secret name exclusively with her son: a key factor in Horus's mythical viability as future occupant of the throne and divine patron of the living pharaoh. Though virtually all of these versions of the myth are relative latecomers to the tradition about Isis, they serve to explain the ascendance of this goddess to a level of importance and veneration that eventually overshadowed that accorded to Ra himself.

Champion of Horus the Avenger

Even though the god Horus could take on a bewildering number of forms, he was at his most popular when in the form of *Hor-sa-eset*—Horus, son of Isis and (the reconstituted) Osiris. As noted, this form of Horus first enters the compendium of his parents' mythology in the murky Delta swamps, where he was born and raised.

One myth describes Horus as a somewhat sickly child, at first. Isis and Nephthys, however, nourished him to great strength through their magically fortified breast-milk. As the result of such specialized care, Horus grew handsome and true. Various gods began to teach him the things all ancient Egyptian princes needed to learn when young: how to kill, maim, and make war. At times, even Osiris was able to rouse himself from the underworld to train his offspring in the ways of battle and, hopefully, to one day wrestle the throne from evil Set.

Though Horus did develop some impressive combat skills, Set could only laugh in derision when the youth first arose to assert his claim to the royal throne. Set's scorn bothered Isis, who clearly hadn't endured all those lean years in the swamplands for naught. Armed with newfound power, the goddess engaged in direct argument with her evil brother. Horus, she contended, deserved the throne by virtue of the right of succession because he was the son of Osiris.

These ancient Egyptian deities would have fit well within the framework of modern society, for Isis and Set did what others today might do in a similar predicament: they took each other to court. Wisely, Isis secured the services of Thoth to represent the interests of Horus. Sadly, the ancient wheels of mythical justice proved to be just as slow and ineffectual as some modern examples. To begin, Isis might have surmised that the entire trial was "fixed" when the judge turned out to be borderline senile *and* a close friend of the defendant. None other than Ra appointed himself chief arbiter of the tribunal—Ra from whom Isis had recently conned that most secret of names. The jury for this farce seems to have been comprised of all the other Egyptian deities, great and small. All of them proved to be fickle or incapable of making unanimous decisions regarding the contentions of Horus and Set. They bickered among themselves over the issues:

Should Horus be King simply by virtue of succession and the wily sorcery of Isis?

Should Set remain Lord because he was older, smarter, stronger, and had practically bribed the incontinent judge? After all, Ra needed the mighty Set to defeat the cosmic serpent, Apophis, who had a penchant for attacking his solar bark as it made its way across the heavens.

None of the gods could decide, even though Thoth used all of his eloquence to persuade the council in favor of young Horus. Even when it seemed he had convinced the majority of the gods, Ra still grumbled and refused to endorse the son of Isis.

They tried everything to reach a satisfactory decision. They asked the esteemed ram-headed god, Banebdjet of Mendes, to give an opinion, but this deity obfuscated and refused to render a verdict. Powerful Neith of Sais was sent a letter seeking her thoughts on the matter, but shunning the limelight, she merely sent a note to the council recommending that Horus be given the throne as long as Set received a compensatory package complete with a couple of aggressive foreign goddesses—Anat and

Astarte—presumably to take the place of Nephthys, who had deserted him. Neith also threatened to make the entire sky fall upon the other gods in catastrophic fashion if her advice was ignored, but Ra was apparently unafraid of her power; he continued to champion Set.

In another version of the myth, the council even conjured-up the ghost of Osiris in order to get *his* opinion. Not surprisingly, he believed that Horus should be given the throne.

The bickering continued, to the frustration of all in attendance. The fury of Isis reached a crescendo and she threatened to put a curse upon all the gods if they didn't reach a decision in her favor. To counter the threat of Isis, Set promised to *murder* all of the gods, one-a-day, if Isis was not ejected from the proceedings. From this point on in the story, Isis was successfully banned from the scene. The deliberations were said to have continued for another eighty years.

Isis—Most Clever of All the Gods

Yet another mythical example of Isis' ability to outwit her foes can be seen in stories relating the subsequent contentions of Horus and Set. Though banned from the council summoned to decide the kingship, Isis plotted to condemn her wicked brother through the agency of his own words. Transforming herself into a withered crone, Isis bribed Anti, the ferryman of the gods, into giving her a ride to the island of the council. Even though Anti had been warned that Isis was at her most powerful when in crone-form, he was quickly swayed by her persuasive words and especially by the gift of a precious ring. He rowed her to the place of meeting.

Knowing that Set was nothing if not a lecherous fiend, Isis transformed herself yet again upon reaching the island. This time, she became an irresistible beauty and managed to catch Set alone as he strolled about. Throwing several come-hither glances, Isis enraptured Set with lust. In return, Set was frantic in his efforts to woo this ravishing damsel. Before allowing any sort of congress, however, Isis distracted the amorous god with a carefully contrived tale of woe.

Suddenly overcome with tears, she claimed to be the widowed wife of a local shepherd whose son had taken over the duty of guarding his deceased father's cattle. She lamented the fact that a total stranger had one day come upon the boy at his task, beaten him, and chased him away, stealing the family's herd. Set reacted to this tale with great anger, so enamored was he by the guise of Isis. He loudly declared that the man who stole the cattle could not possibly get away with the crime, especially since the boy was the clear heir to his father's property. He assured the weeping woman that the law was firmly on the side of the *son's* interests.

This was all that Isis needed to hear. In a flash, she changed herself into a falcon and flew to the upper branches of an acacia tree, mocking the stunned Set and rejoicing in the success of her trickery. By his very statement, the god had condemned his own unjust usurpation of the throne of Osiris! Faced with such self-damnation, Set could merely run away, bemoaning his stupidity to Ra, who had to admit that Isis had gotten the better of them all once again.

Isis the Beheaded?

Despite this ruse on the part of Isis, the throne had not been secured for Horus. The trial continued until Set contended (with the strange encouragement of Hathor) that the only certain way to settle the matter was to have an old-fashioned battle. That, no doubt, would prove which god had the mettle to rule the Two Lands. Set's plan was simple: he and Horus would turn themselves into hippos and dive into the bottom of a lake until such time that one or the other could no longer breathe and had to rise to the surface. Three months underwater was deemed the minimum. The more durable of the two, the one who could stay down the longest, would take the throne. The rather naïve assembly of gods agreed that this was indeed a very good idea. Even Horus, in a burst of bravery, figured he could outlast his uncle in the swamps.

Isis knew better, however. She knew that Set was at his mightiest and most merciless when in hippo-form. Once he had cornered Horus in the water, her son would be finished. The boy wouldn't stand a chance against the sharper, more experienced tusks of his uncle. Elements of this myth must have certainly come from the ancients witnessing the ferocity of adult male hippos when on-the-attack against younger, newly introduced male members of the herd.

Nevertheless, the grossly mismatched rivals duly transformed themselves and dove-in among the lily pads and lotuses. Little did they realize that mighty Isis was hidden among the reeds along the riverbank, armed with an enchanted harpoon. Her goal was to hurl the thing at Set before the brute had a chance to mutilate her son. As the inevitable battle got underway, Isis's aim proved a bit inaccurate amid the confusion. Her first strike punctured Horus instead of Set. The youth bellowed in agony and Isis quickly used a spell to call the harpoon back into her hands. Then she made another strike, this time finding the desired target. Now *Set* was the one screaming in pain, appealing to his sister's deepest sentiments to set him free. The ploy worked, for Isis was moved by something in Set's nostalgic plea. In a fit of sadness (and merciful poor judgment), she called the harpoon out of her brother. This change of sentiment did not set well with Horus, who had obviously gained the upper "hoof." Storming the riverbank, he confronted his mother, calling her a traitor to his cause. In the myth, it is said that:

As before a panther from the South, Isis fled from Horus for her very life.

Her attempt to escape the enraged Horus was futile. Seizing an axe, Horus chopped his mother's head off in a rage. Resourceful as ever, Isis made use of her magic and transformed herself into a statue of flint at the very instant she would have perished. All of the other gods ran off in a frantic search to find her head, which Horus had flung away in disgust. Meanwhile, the headless, rigid condition did not deter the adamant Isis, who presumably bumped into many a tree while making her way back to the scene of the tribunal. Upon arrival, she mingled rather conspicuously among the company of gods, prompting Ra himself to deadpan:

"Exactly who *is* this headless woman in our midst?"

Once again, Thoth came to the rescue, placing the temporary head of a cow upon the shoulders of Isis. This scene was most likely a mythical reflection of Isis' hallowed role as the mother-cow of the sacred Apis bull (an incarnation of Osiris at Saqqara) and later of her widespread usurpation of Hathor's personality.

Knowing he had committed a serious mistake by cutting off the head of his mother, the most powerful sorceress in the world, Horus ran away into the mountains as the gods called for his punishment. Ra fiendishly suggested that Set should be the one to exact revenge and the eager god wasted little time in finding the boy. He promptly scratched Horus' eyes out and left him alone in a blind daze, moaning at such misfortune. Luckily, Hathor came to his rescue with a magic potion made of gazelle's milk. This she poured into the eyes of the embattled god and restored his vision.

In the end, Isis didn't hold a grudge against her son and, after the two reconciled, she urged him to resume his battle against Set. Several confrontations followed, but even though each god seemed to claim victory on occasion, the other always found a way to escape and return to fight another day.

Alas, even an ill-advised race in "stone boats" (of all things) was unable to produce a clear victor in the ongoing contentions. Horus wisely fashioned his racing boat out of buoyant cedar and painted it to *look* as if it were made of stone. However, when Set's genuine stone-made boat sank straightaway, the angry god simply reverted back into hippo form and tried to capsize his nephew.

The Triumph of Isis and Horus

After yet another round of flying harpoons, the council of gods decided to call once more upon the shadowy Osiris to speak his mind and settle the tiresome matter forever. Why everyone was unwilling to accept his judgment the first time is uncertain, but it should be understood that these various strains of Egyptian myth are often rather contradictory and confusing.

Osiris didn't bother to leave the underworld at this summons. Instead, he opted to send a letter to the council in which he scorned the entire lot for being such indecisive idiots. He also took the opportunity to remind them that *he* was the god with the most influence in the universe. Indeed, he reminded them that the entire agricultural cycle of the Two Lands was dependent upon his power. By association, so was the survival of every man woman and child who supported the pharaoh, who in turn guaranteed the sustenance of worship to the immortals. If Horus was not awarded the throne, he warned, there would be serious consequences.

The gods of the council knew this, of course, which is presumably why most of them had been somewhat partial to Horus from the beginning, despite their fear of Set. Ra, however, was not the least bit impressed with the ultimatum of Osiris. The addled god fired-off a missive of his own, implying that Osiris was not as vital to the cosmic scheme of things as he thought he was, and warning the dark god to stay out of the matter. Unperturbed, Osiris sent a final, unambiguous threat. If Horus were denied the throne, Osiris would, as Lord of the Underworld, unleash the terrifying beasts known as the "Ferocious of Faces." These demons, all of whom were at his command, had the power (by sheer numbers) to carry away any god or goddess who took the side of Set.

Mindful of this harrowing alternative, the gods finally agreed that Horus should be given the throne of his father and rule as Lord of the Two Lands. An appropriately Horus-harpooned Set was apprehended and dragged before the council of gods in chains by none other than Isis, who was herself finally vindicated. Thereafter, Set was restricted to the important duty of slaying the Apophis serpent that assailed Ra's solar barge and was otherwise banished to the desert outskirts and seashores of the delta, where he resided with his new foreign consorts, Astarte and Anat. Horus became the avenger he was destined to become and took his place in majesty—a mythical reflection of the historical fact that *he* was the first of the ancient deities to be so closely associated with the pharaoh, who was for all purposes his avatar. Clearly, the Egyptians felt the need to explain all of these realities by virtue of myth, and we are all the richer for their attempts.

Isis—Great Goddess of the People

With the onset of the New Kingdom, such mythical perseverance made Isis irresistible to the spiritual sensibilities of the everyday Egyptian. Women and men alike identified with her harrowing grief at the murder of Osiris and they wept along with her when annual "Passion Plays" were enacted at Busiris, Abydos, and a great many other locales throughout Egypt. Women could relate to the travails of Isis as a mother struggling to protect, feed, and nurture her baby, while men praised her determination, ferocity, and loyalty in raising an avenger for Osiris.

Indeed, the image of a wife who used great cunning and sorcery to support both husband and son may have touched the male Egyptian psyche in ways that other goddess cults could not. For this reason, Isis possessed the perfect combination of attributes that made her veneration truly widespread. It is not surprising that, after the end of the New Kingdom, as these myths became more elaborate, Isis started to become more beloved than any other Egyptian deity, including her husband and son.

Owing to this popularity, the Isis cult began to swiftly absorb the cults and temples of other goddesses, great and small. Everywhere, the local town-goddess could be viewed as just another form of Isis, while local cosmologies and myths were swiftly tailored to fit Isaic structures. Cultic identification with deities like Renenutet of the Fayyum kept Egyptian religious focus upon the life-giving, fertility aspects of the Isis-figure within the framework of the Osirian myth, preserving her ancient identity as an agricultural deity. In this capacity, hard-working Egyptians had little trouble seeing the "Tears of Isis" (and sometimes of Nephthys) as a cause of the annual inundation. Isis's struggles on behalf of Horus and Osiris were equated with the human struggle to subdue the earth and cause it to bear healthy crops year after year.

The domain of Isis extended to the firmament, even at an early date. She had long been equated with the star Sothis, just as Osiris was identified with the Orion constellation. The annual "rising" of these stars in the heavens was not only a harbinger of the coming flood, but a cause for national celebration. Above all, Isis was a goddess of the people, on the side of the people. Egyptians took comfort in her tender embrace and felt comfortable laying their problems at her feet with full confidence that she would answer their prayers. Isis was a goddess who was accessible to her worshippers in every phase of their lives—from birth, to childhood, to marriage, to death, and especially afterward, when she promised protection in the underworld along with her sister Nephthys, enfolded in golden wings and guided into the presence of her fearsome husband.

Though small cult-rooms of Isis were numerous in temples of other gods from at least the Middle Kingdom Period, she remained largely a beloved household divinity. It was only with the onset of the New Kingdom and the Late Period that significant temple structures seem to have been raised in her honor. The great Osirian Temple of Seti I at Abydos was dedicated to many gods, but to seven in particular; Isis—the chief Osirian goddess—was one of them. Pharaoh Amasis supposedly raised a vast temple for Isis at Memphis, where her popularity rivaled that of the local goddess Sekhmet. Amasis and Nectanebo I also started sanctuaries for Isis on the little island of Philae near the Nubian border and the frothy First Cataract of the Nile.

The island of Philae would come into its own as a great Osirian cult center during Ptolemaic times. Before that, Pharaoh Nectanebo II (360-343 BCE) started an even greater temple for Isis at Per-Hebitet (Behbeit), as noted. Built entirely of Aswan granite and decorated with some of the finest reliefs of the period, this sanctuary seems to have been linked with a "family" temple of Osiris, Isis, Nephthys, and Horus at neighboring Busiris. The Behbeit Temple served the purpose of enabling Isis to perform the annual restorative rituals and to "lay down the [Osirian] offerings" needed for the success of the annual fertility cycle. When the Greeks gained control of this region they dubbed the town "Isisopolis." It remained the northern stronghold of the Isis cult until the temple apparently imploded during an earthquake sometime before 80 CE. It makes for a rather gorgeous heap of blocks even to this day; attempts to reconstruct and rebuild the temple are reputedly in the works.

The Rise of Euro-Isis

Greeks before and after the thunderous coming of Alexander the Great proved to be just as attracted to Isis as the native Egyptians. Unlike many of the other deities, her qualities demonstrated a more universal appeal—one capable of transcending the decline of the overall Egyptian culture and empire. Gradually, foreign settlers in Egypt became devotees of the Osirian cult, giving its associated gods various "Macedonian makeovers." Under the patronage of Ptolemy I Soter, Osiris transformed into the rather Dionysian deity Serapis and, along with Isis, ruled the vast religious panorama that existed in Egypt's glorious new capital, Alexandria. Several fine temples were built in this city specifically for Isis and her worship was successfully exported to many other communities along the Mediterranean. Merchants, traders, and other travelers were eager to introduce the locals back home to such an esoteric and enchanting foreign goddess.

Though Europe in Greco-Roman times was a virtual supermarket of religious trends and cults, Isis the merciful, universal Mother rose to the top of the heap in succeeding centuries. Her shrines began to pop-up everywhere: Delos; Corinth, Cyprus; Tithoria; Thira; Crete; Ephesus; Athens, Pompeii; Sicily; Naples—you name the town, Isis was there. The Euro-temples and rites retained *some* trappings of the Egyptian heritage while the roles of Isis as healer, giver of eternal life, patroness of mothers, and protectress of seafarers were emphasized. In the past, Isis has rightfully been described as an Egyptian lunar goddess. While her ancient cult did have such associations, her lunar identity was far more prominently forged under Greco-Roman influence, via close connections with deities like Artemis.

Other celestial qualities were emphasized, too. Titles like Stella Maris, or "Star of the Sea" were taken directly from the cult of Isis and applied to the later veneration of the Virgin Mary, as were the epithets "Our Lady," "Queen of Heaven," and a bit more arguably, "Mother of [the] God." It is an interesting coincidence that feasts, festivals, and rites of mysterious initiation blossomed around the time Mary's Son was first making a religious impact in the Roman Empire. The fact that Isis, like Jesus, promised eternal happiness in the afterlife did not hurt Isis's marketability. This quality was something the established state cults of Greece and Rome could not offer with similar confidence.

Isis Conquers the Eternal City

Though political leaders were wary of the Isis cult and its exotic flavor, they were unable to halt the juggernaut. Lucius Cornelius Sulla appears to have introduced her cult to the suspicious Roman citizenry around 86 BCE. Isis had already been worshiped in Puteoli, Ostia, and other Roman suburbs for some time, but it's important to realize that the Senate was rather choosy about the gods it allowed to receive worship within the imperial city's walls. Once established, the cult of Isis gained immediate traction among the common folk, though Roman officials and the nobility largely held it in contempt due to deteriorating political relations with Egypt.

Authorities eager to suppress the goddess destroyed her Roman shrines in 54, 50, and 48 BCE, but such common appeal only succeeded in making Isis even more intriguing to the populace. Demand had been so great that a sizeable temple was built for her in Rome around 43 BCE, instantly becoming one of the city's most popular sanctuaries.

Despite obstacles, Isis-worship remained strong in Rome in subsequent decades, though it was regularly dealt blows by scandal. For example, the Cleopatra/Marc-Antony debacle didn't help her cause. At some point, the emperor Augustus prohibited her worship, but Isis only waxed in popularity following the proscription. Finally, the government relented when the cult began to win followers among the upper classes. Isis thrived again until her priests were involved in a shocking scandal around the year 19 CE.

The Persecution of Isis

The writer Josephus recounts a rather shady event in which the dog-faced god, Anubis, appears to have gotten his mistress into a bit of trouble. According to the Jewish historian, a revered noblewoman named Paulina was duped into spending a night in the temple of Isis so that she might experience some sort of mystical communion with the goddess. Little did she know that one of her admirers had bribed a priest and disguised himself with the ritual mask of Anubis in an attempt to make certain untoward advances.

This deception scandalized the entire city of Rome and prompted Emperor Tiberius to butcher the entire priesthood of Isis and raze her sanctuary to the ground. After this, Isis was widely ridiculed and her shaved-headed clerics were considered immoral. Over the next several years, her shrines were routinely sabotaged and her statues abducted and tossed into the Tiber River, but the cult did not die. Amazingly, the fury subsided after a period of time and another massive temple to Isis was erected on the Campus Martius in 39 CE. From that point onward—with only the occasional hiccup—Isis became the most popular goddess in the Eternal City.

With Egypt solidly in Roman hands and cultic restrictions relaxed, Isis gained followers from every social class. Under the auspices of the far-reaching empire, her worship received an enormous promotional push. In the first few centuries of the Christian era, temples of Isis were built in France, Germany, Austria, Spain, Hungary, and even distant Britain.

The Battle for Europe's Soul

In the first four centuries of the Christian millennium, the battle for the Empire's unified soul seems to have been a multi-faceted competition between the Isis cult, Christianity, the worship of the Persian god, Mithras, and an assortment of other Mediterranean mystery cults like those of Cybele and Dionysus. While all quite distinct and different, each of these cults shared an intriguing number of characteristics, including some form of the promise of eternal life.

Though extremely powerful, Mithraism was perhaps the most limited of the cults because it was almost exclusively a man's religion, claiming the majority of its devotees among the Roman military. The state deities—Jupiter, Minerva, etc.—all survived through the graces (and funds) of the aristocracy, but Christianity appealed mainly to the poorer working classes, who were abundant. Increasingly, Romans of many backgrounds came to be impressed by the zeal of Christian adherents willing to suffer martyrdom for their faith, but they were not quite as willing to adopt the yoke of Christianity's strict moral demands. To be certain, the Roman mindset had come to appreciate a distinct favor for selective moral standards and general free-spiritedness.

The Isis cult combined the earthy, exotic spirituality the pagan population craved along with the tender, salvific promises seen in competing Christianity. In this sense, Isis worship might best be viewed as an ideal bridge between the malaise of the state cults and the scrupulous zeal of the new Christian religion. Christianity, however, proved itself to be the more adaptable faith in terms of doctrinal, social, and organizational development. It won its fair share of friends in high places and learned to woo the pagan constituency away by fighting fire with fire. Christian teachers were wise enough to see that European spirituality was vastly different from the Judaic origins of their faith in that it placed great emphasis upon the maternal qualities of divinity. Accordingly, the Christian Church slowly began to encourage the uplifting of its own built-in feminine resource—the Virgin Mary. By honoring Mary as a wholesome, ascetic alternative to the ribald pagan goddesses, Christians played into the more assiduously moral circles of Roman society and contemporaneous philosophical ideals.

The Decline of Isis…and Paganism

Once Christianity had the political strength to spread its doctrine via Emperor Constantine and his patronage, the glory days of Isis began to wane. When later emperors like Theodosius forced Christianity upon the Empire in the late fourth century, it wasn't terribly difficult for most of the people to switch their allegiance from Mithras to Jesus or from Isis to the Virgin. Throughout Europe, only fanatical or provincial worshipers refused to abandon the rites and temples of Isis. These factions found themselves increasingly marginalized. Even so, some temples of the goddess continued to flourish—at Soissons in France and likewise in Paris, which may have even taken its name from a tribal variant of the Egyptian sacred name "Per-Isis." This goddess knew how to leave her mark.

While Euro-Isis was on the decline, much of the same was happening in Egypt. The story of the end of ancient Egyptian culture, mythology, and religion is essentially a story about Isis. While the classic civilization of native pharaohs had ended long before with the coming of Alexander and his string of Ptolemaic successors, the cult of Isis in Egypt had always clung boldly to its traditional heritage.

To fully comprehend the fall of Isis, it is important to remember that Christianity took root more enthusiastically in Egypt than anywhere else in the ancient Mediterranean world. A veritable war brewed for years in Alexandria between followers of Isis and Jesus, particularly in the fourth century. In Rome, around 394, Nichomachus Flavianus hoped that a massive Isis-Fest would kindle his great "Pagan Revival," but the movement flopped and lasted a paltry three months. A few years later, in 397, Christian fanatics smashed the glorious "Serapaeum" and other Isis shrines at Alexandria—a score they had been keen to settle for over one hundred years.

At Thebes, the gargantuan temple of Amun-Ra at Karnak was filled with squatters and goats, its cult no longer relevant or powerful enough to support (or be supported by) a flagging economy. Abydos was by then a virtual ghost-town, most of its hallowed Osirian significance having been transferred to distant Philae a few centuries earlier. Devotees of the old gods found themselves pushed to the outskirts and frontiers by Coptic Christian zeal, or forced to mingle the memories of the old gods with new cults of the Christian saints—much in the fashion that more modern religious phenomena like Santeria attempt in Catholic nations today. With the old religion pushed to the brink, it is not surprising that shrines like that of Amun at far-off Siwah Oasis and of Isis at holy, remote Philae survived the longest.

At Philae, ancient Egyptian religion breathed its last. Perhaps the final, extant hieroglyphic inscription was carved there in the fifth century, long after "Egyptian" had become a dead language, known only (and barely) to a handful of watered-down priests. The gorgeous temple of Isis became the last bastion of the old worship. Some believers still made secret pilgrimages to Philae from various parts of the Mediterranean, long after most of the people had joined the Coptic Church. By the late fifth century, however, with the legalistic tide of Christianity rising from all sides, Philae found its only adherents among the various Nubian tribes in the southern wilderness.

There, clans like the Blemmyes held fast to the Temple of Isis and their numbers were strong enough to win certain allowances from the strict Byzantine/Christian government. Even after other pagan sanctuaries had long been closed, destroyed by edict, or converted into makeshift Christian churches, the Blemmyes were allowed to take the cult statues of Isis deep into the Nubian jungle for annual visits.

This practice lingered for a time, but once Christian preachers made inroads in Nubia and the tribe's power began to decline, Isis was finished. Sometime between 535 and 545 the Emperor Justinian gave official orders for the famous temple of Isis at Philae to be closed. He sent his general, Narses, to chase any remaining priests from the sanctuary and jail them for heresy. The cult-statues in residence at Philae were hauled away to distant Constantinople. What became of them no one knows.

This act marked the official end of the ancient Egyptian Isis cult and the end of semi-authentic ancient Egyptian religion. If, as some scholars speculate, Isis was worshipped in secret by scattered Nubian tribes until the Muslim occupation (which would all but obliterate Christianity), we may surmise that she bore little resemblance to the powerful goddess that had once conquered numerous nations.

REMNANTS OF ISIS: Isis can be found throughout Egypt, in virtually every temple ruin. You can't miss her. Her sacred island of Philae, the "Pearl of Egypt" near the Aswan High Dam, is a *must.* Take a mesmerizing daytime trip and spend a couple of hours wandering through her exquisite Greco-Roman temple complex. After dark, visitors will not see the temples in full splendor, but are nevertheless treated to a bewitching light-show that has its own atmospheric merits.

Maat

Chief Role: Goddess of Truth and Cosmic Balance
Chief Title: "Mistress of the Balance of the Two Worlds"
Cult Centers: Thebes, Memphis

Though the goddess Maat has been described by many as a mere "concept" in the pharaonic religious tradition, nothing could be further from the truth. While there were indeed highly conceptualized qualities crucial to this goddess and her personality, she was one of the most important deities in the entire pantheon and the object of a distinct cult of her own at numerous junctures in ancient Egyptian history.

To say that Maat was simply the "Goddess of Truth" is problematic. While she could be regarded as the embodiment of Truth, and was thought to have sprung from the primordial Chaos along with the glorious Atum-Ra, Maat and the forces of Chaos are inextricably linked. Atum allegedly used Maat as a creative tool in the ordering of creation and, for this reason, she is called the "Mistress of the Balance of the Two Worlds." Maat brought a sense of order to the universe, not simply moral truth. In this capacity, she was given a permanent seat of honor on Atum-Ra's solar bark. There, she spent Eternity commandeering the forces that fostered harmony in the lives of Egyptians and nature itself. She was linked to the very maintenance of existence. Her reputation as the steadfast associate of Ra or Atum-Ra would last throughout ancient Egyptian religious history, earning her the typical (but in this case quite appropriate) epithet, "Daughter of Ra.

Goddess of Cosmic Equilibrium

As noted, the Egyptian theologians appear to have considered Maat to exemplify a state of balance, rather than simple moral or social honesty—though morals were a key part of that balance. Maat represented a complementary union of the often polarized forces at work in the visible and invisible worlds: feast and famine; happiness and misery; life and death; good and evil; flood and drought; war and peace. People honored and preserved Maat by seeking to maintain that cosmic equilibrium within the context of their daily lives. When individuals (or society as a whole) strayed too far from the preservation of Maat, the shadowy specter of Chaos was said to be unleashed, little by little, upon the kingdom.

How did the Egyptians "preserve" Maat in a cultic sense? Foremost, Pharaoh himself had the chief responsibility to see that Maat was preserved according to temple rituals. If Maat were neglected, the entire nation was believed subject to catastrophe and the gods themselves were unable to function. This is why temple reliefs of the Pharaoh so often depict him offering a small figure of Maat to various important deities as "proof" that he was upholding *his* promise to preserve all that the goddess represented. By accepting Pharaoh's gift of Maat, the resident temple god was thereby assuring (in a truly magical sense) that the state of harmony between deity, mortal, earth, and cosmos would be maintained.

Goddess of the Hall of Two Truths

The role of Maat as representative of cosmic harmony (for the common good) led to a crucial auxiliary task in the Judgment Halls of the Dead. Here, Maat operated under the auspices of Osiris himself. Associated with each other even in the Dynasty V Pyramid Texts, Osiris and Maat worked in tandem for the benefit of Duat and its occupants. Maat assumed the role of a reassuring hostess, gently leading the newly departed soul through the murky corridors and treacherous gates of the Afterlife.

Before the final meeting with Osiris, a personal judgment of the deceased was required. From at least the New Kingdom, Egyptians believed that Maat played a singular role in securing a measure of eternal bliss for the dead. The underworld precinct where judgment took place was even called "The Hall of the Two Maats," representing both elements of Truth and, in some ways, perhaps the dual figures of Isis and Nephthys, who were often called "The Two Maat Goddesses." In this Hall, the heart of the deceased was placed on one end of a great scale to see whether or not its earthly deeds were worthy of eternal happiness. The human heart was weighed against a miniature form of the goddess Maat herself, placed at the opposite end of the scale. Only a decent balance would result in everlasting life for the deceased. Any discrepant heart was met with rather swift disposal. In that instance, the "Devourer"—a hideous monster-goddess called Ammut—waited eagerly to eat any heart that failed to make the grade.

In some temple and papyrus records, the mere symbol of Maat—an ostrich feather?—was placed on the scale by dog-headed Anubis. Again, it must be stressed that Maat's underworld duties stemmed directly from the concept of her role as a reflection of right-hearted living and its implications for harmony with the entire universe. If Egyptians maintained that delicate balance, they would take their rightful place in eternal happiness with Osiris.

The Cult of Maat

As both a stylized concept *and* a personal figure in the Egyptian pantheon, it is difficult to determine how much independent cult was accorded to Maat. On the one hand, every Egyptian was mindful of her significance and the pharaoh was most concerned with her satisfaction. Yet, there existed no widespread temple-cults devoted to this important goddess. This may be due to the fact that her rites were already part-and-parcel of the worship of every god in *every* temple.

The goddess did, however, possess her own sanctuaries. There was a cult of Maat at Thebes; her small temple there was a subsidiary shrine of the great complex devoted to the war-god, Montu. She was also apparently worshipped at Memphis, where a temple dating from the time of Seti I may have been dedicated to her rites. In Memphis and elsewhere, the title "Prophet of Maat" could apply to viziers and judges as much as it could have applied to actual cultic priests of the goddess.

The only extant temple of Maat is found in the ruins of Deir Al-Madinah near the Theben necropolis. In this small but elegant temple, Maat had her own naos and cult image while sharing the sacred complex equally with Hathor, Imhotep, and a deified version of Pharaoh Amenophis. Although the Deir Al-Madinah temple is Ptolemaic in origin, Maat's cultic kinship with Hathor was much more ancient, stemming from their mutual proximity to Ra, as well as a belief that, once again, Maat represented a point of balance—this time between vicious Sekhmet and ribald Hathor in their respective and often arbitrary personalities as the “Distant [Raging] Goddess” and the “Joyful Goddess.” In this sense, Maat could be viewed as the personification of the ideal compromise represented by a beneficent inundation, or “good flood.”

While Maat was a solitary and potentially abstract goddess, ancient theologians often associated her with various other deities, as we have seen. Though there is little evidence that she possessed cult images in the temples of Thoth, Maat was sometimes said to be that god’s consort. We know not whether this caused any friction between Maat and Thoth’s primary consort, Seshat, but any protest on the latter’s part would have been futile.

After all, it is never advisable to trifle with the Truth.

Mertseger

Chief Role: Avenger of the Righteous Dead
Chief Title: "Mistress of the Peak of the West," "She Who Loves the Silence"
Cult Centers: Deir Al-Madinah

Mertseger is one of the most mysterious goddesses in the ancient Egyptian pantheon. This is fitting for a deity whose epithet was the enigmatic "She Who Loves the Silence." Mertseger's love for silence did not stem from a desire for solitude, but from the stark isolation of her reputed dwelling place, the holy "Peak of the West."

This rock formation, naturally shaped into pyramid-form by the elements overlooking the Valley of the Kings, must have seemed ready-made for divine residence of some sort. Hathor was highly revered in this lofty spot and throughout the region of Deir Al-Madinah. Nearby, there dwelled working families that constructed the royal tombs. Like Hathor, Mertseger was a local goddess associated with all the mystery bound-up with the west bank of the Nile as the "entrance" to the Underworld. Toward the end of the Middle Kingdom, Mertseger actually usurped the primacy of Hathor as special protectress of the Theban necropolis.

Patroness of Tomb Builders

In addition to being a fearsome protectress of the deceased, Mertseger was primarily a goddess who watched over the communities that built and maintained the necropolis. The workers and their families looked to her for special favor by erecting household votive shrines in her honor. Mertseger's importance to the people of Deir Al-Madinah is also evident by numerous votive stelae discovered over the years throughout the region.

The task of building and guarding the royal and noble tombs of the Theban necropolis was fraught with danger and intrigue. Thievery and corruption were always a serious threat in the Valley, especially toward the end of the Middle Kingdom. For this reason, Mertseger acquired a reputation as a particularly vicious goddess, an avenging serpent able to find and punish liars and thieves, break curses, and heal the afflictions of her devotees. One ancient hymn to Mertseger assures her followers that: "The Peak of the West is appeased…if only one calls out her name."

Though the anger of Mertseger toward evildoers was often likened to that of a raging lioness, much in the manner of Sekhmet, the goddess was normally represented in her usual serpentine form. This motif led to her association with the popular harvest deity, Renenutet, who was a more motherly figure in the often jam-packed Theban parade of underworld divinities. Many tombs in the

Valley of the Kings and Queens testify to Mertseger's enormous prestige. In the tombs of Ramses IX and the Prophet Userhet, for example, she is seen fit to stand alongside the great Amun-Ra-Harakhte as the souls of the dead make the required afterlife offerings.

Though for centuries Mertseger enjoyed great veneration in one of Egypt's most thriving and crucial worker-communities, her fame did not extend terribly far beyond the boundaries of Thebes. She is sometimes depicted as wearing the Red Crown of Lower Egypt, but this may have been due to her identification with Renenutet of the Fayyum Oasis. A fusion of Hathor-Mertseger was attested at Deir El-Bahri, in the funerary temple of Hatshepsut, and the goddess may have been the object of a late cult at Esna, though this remains uncertain. When royal burials in the Valley of the Kings came largely to a halt with the close of the New Kingdom, Mertseger vanished with the worker communities that had so honored her. Thus it was that Mertseger faded a bit into history and into the silence she so greatly craved. Curiously, the "Peak of the West" is said by some Egyptians to be haunted by a vengeful spirit to this very day.

REMNANTS OF MERTSEGER: Look for this exquisite goddess painted in the accessible tombs of the Valley of the Kings and Queens. Above all, get at least one snapshot of her mythical dwelling-place, the pyramid-like "Peak of the West," which still keeps watch over the resting places of the ancient dead.

Meskhenet

Chief Role: Goddess of Destiny and Protectress of Women in Labor
Chief Title: "The Cubit with a Head"
Cult Centers: "Birth House" temples in primary temple precincts throughout Egypt

Judging from some temple reliefs, Meskhenet may have been the most physically challenged of the great Egyptian goddesses; after all, it must have been difficult having a body composed of nothing but a couple of bricks and a head. Yet, Meskhenet did not need much more than that to fulfill her pivotal role as a protectress of women during the process of childbirth.

In truth, the "brick," or cubed body of Meskhenet, is a symbol pertaining to the traditional birthing-seat upon which Egyptian woman positioned themselves when delivering a newborn. Though perhaps all ancient Egyptian goddesses were invoked at some time or another as guardians during pregnancy and birth, Meskhenet was one of the more prominent and accessible, due to her keen identification with the birthing bricks. She is also prominent in childbirth folklore and myth dating from at least the Middle Kingdom.

The Dancing Goddesses

According to a tale preserved in Papyrus Westcar, there once lived a woman named Rudedet, who was the wife of the First Prophet of the god Ra. A powerful sorcerer named Dedi had prophesied to Pharaoh Khufu that Rudedet's three sons would one day rule the land of Egypt and come to be considered the sons of Ra himself. Before Rudedet gave birth to the boys—whose names were to be Useref, Sahure, and Neferkara—Ra decided that his progeny should receive an appropriate welcome into the world. Thus, he summoned the goddesses Isis, Nephthys, Heqet, and Meskhenet, commanding them to pay the expectant mother an honorary visit. Ra reminded the four goddesses that such a visit would bode well for them; when the children grew up to become great rulers, the temples of Isis, Nephthys, Heqet, and Meskhenet would be properly maintained and appointed.

Realizing the importance of ingratiating themselves, the four goddesses departed the divine realm and paid a visit to Rudedet. To keep themselves from stunning the mother-to-be with the majesty of their divine auras, the goddesses transformed themselves into a quartet of dancing girls. Enlisting the god Khnum as their porter, they arrived at the home of Rudedet and her husband, the First Prophet of Ra. There, each goddess played a unique role in helping Rudedet deliver her triplets. Isis stood before Rudedet to receive the newborn, Nephthys stood behind to strengthen her, Heqet imparted the breath of life to each baby, and Meskhenet solemnly prophesied the fabulous destiny of each child. After this, whirling in a blaze of revelry, the goddesses danced for Rudedet and her astonished husband to the musical accompaniment of the affable Khnum. In a spirit of thanks, Rudedet gave the goddesses a bushel of barley and the divine visitors took their leave.

Meskhenet's unique role as prophetess in the myth secured for her a function as harbinger of the newborn child's lifelong happiness and successful destiny. Obviously, with the threats of famine, disease, and numerous other complications that afflicted infants of the time, Meskhenet was called upon to thwart the designs of evil that were always lurking at the heels of human existence. Reality was often grim in the ancient world; Egypt was no exception to the extremely high rate of infant mortality.

Perhaps for this reason, Meskhenet was also invoked as an intercessor for the dead with the other underworld gods, in order that the dead might be "born" into the Afterlife with success, even if their worldly emergence was less than promising. In the *Book of the Dead,* Meskhenet appears in the Hall of the Two Truths at the side of Renenutet, another goddess highly skilled in midwifery. In the Late Period and Ptolemaic times, Meskhenet was appropriately linked with Shay, a very popular male deity who decided individual human destiny in oracular fashion (via his priests).

In temple art, Meskhenet was often depicted as a woman with a strange, double-looped symbol atop her head and was not always confined to such cubic form; she can be fully anthropomorphic at times. Her headdress has variously been identified as the fertile shoot of a palm-frond or even as some form of uterine symbol. Though she was primarily a household goddess, with household shrines, she could be an independent personality in certain temples belonging to other goddesses throughout Egypt. It is likely that she possessed some sanctuary of her own, but little trace of any significant cult remains. Rather, in temples dedicated to Hathor, Meskhenet seems to occupy a particularly prominent position as both a deity in her own right and as a quadruple "form" of the beloved host goddess. Indeed, an auxiliary cult-statue of Meskhenet appears to have been tended by priests in the great temple at Dendera and reliefs of the goddess are not uncommon throughout the inner chapels of that edifice.

REMNANTS OF MESKHENET: Finding this goddess at Dendara will be a challenge to the intrepid wanderer amid the overwhelming inscriptions of that enormous complex. Meskhenet, however, appears more obviously in small "Birth House" temples *(mammisi)* that were associated with larger cult-temples, particularly during the Ptolemaic period. These peripteral sanctuaries were devoted to the cult of “birthing” the offspring of the chief temple goddess and the pharaohs who patronized the edifice. In such an environment, Meskhenet is often represented as a conglomerate goddess with other deities or, as noted, The Four Meskhenets—a powerful, multi-form midwife hearkening back to the original charm of the legend of Rudedet and her dancing visitors. Philae’s birth-house and the classic birth-scenes of Hatshepsut at Deir el-Bahri are good places to find this divinity.

Mut

Chief Role: Universal Mother-Warrior and Goddess of Thebes
Chief Title: "Mistress of Asheru"
Cult Centers: Thebes (Karnak & Luxor), Deir el-Medineh, etc.

In the Egyptian language, the word *mwt* could mean "mother," but in very ancient usage it could be represented by the vulture hieroglyph. Though this might seem like a confusion of images, the two are not as disparate as one might surmise. Egyptian goddesses could be quite mercurial—Mut was no exception.

In villages on the outskirts of Thebes during the Middle Kingdom, one of the most important local deities bore the name "Mut," and one of her motifs was sometimes understood to be the vulture. Keep in mind that the ancient Egyptians considered this bird to be a symbol of maternal protection, apparently unperturbed by the creature's ugliness and taste for carrion. With her watchful eyes and massive wingspan, the mother vulture could hide her offspring from enemies and the harsh heat of the desert sun. She could also swoop down from the sky and systematically eliminate the rotting carcasses of kills cast aside by satiated predators. It was apparently in this latter sense that Mut moved-in and all but ousted the goddess Amaunet to become the primary "companion" of Amun from at least Dynasty XVIII (1539-1295).

Greatest Goddess of Thebes

With the possible exception of bulky Ipet (a form of the hippopotamus-goddess Taweret), Mut was probably the most ancient goddess of the Theban region. She certainly became the most popular. Before her priesthood finagled the choice cultic alliance with the worship of Amun, Mut was a local goddess from nearby Megen. After becoming Thebes's rising mother-figure and protectress, some eventual union was necessary between her cult and the cult of the ever-more-powerful Amun, chief god of the Theban pharaohs.

As her veneration developed, Mut was perhaps configured as a conglomerate goddess formed by a collision between the powerful Memphite Sekhmet from the North, and the tutelary deity Nekhbet from the South, at El Kab. The lioness was Mut's favored form, however, and she is rarely depicted in the guise of a vulture. Amun's ascension to become "King of the Gods" made him an absorber of the great god Ptah of Memphis, so Mut naturally took her place as "Queen of the Gods" and also as a replacement for Sekhmet at Thebes, at least as far as the State Cult was concerned. While it is debatable that Mut was more of a wife than complementary companion-deity, the divine duo of Thebes completed a family unit by "adopting" a local lunar deity, Khons, particularly as Mut's son, forming arguably the most powerful religious triad in Egypt for centuries.

Though it was likely from the assimilated Sekhmet that Mut acquired her lioness features, her reputed qualities as a hermaphrodite are believed to stem from an ancient superstition that the vulture was able to impregnate itself. This trait secured for Mut a double importance. She could be viewed as a self-contained creative power and also as a raging lioness accompanying Pharaoh and his legions into battle. One hymn to Mut extols her (of course) as the "Eye of Ra," and celebrates the fact that "her aggression is turned against rebels, and her appetite for blood against the desert peoples." Another link with the lovable Bastet could offer Mut a middle-ground between opposing personalities, but her generative importance extended beyond efficient motherhood. Obscure references in several ancient texts indicate that Mut was considered instrumental in the creation of all forms of life. This designation allowed her to assume the aura of an "Architect of the Universe"—a role precious few Egyptian goddesses possessed. Only Neith (with whom Mut was also sometimes associated at Thebes), a few others, and much later, Isis, were widely accorded this power.

Mut's Theban image, however, remained largely that of a protective, triumphant mother. Here the relationship with the pharaoh was emphasized. Theban pharaohs looked to Mut with special affection and were careful to adorn her glorious temple in the Asheru district of the city with riches appropriate to her status. Seti II and Ramses II were notable restorers and benefactors of this renowned institution.

Mut's importance at Thebes was never lost on the common people, either. Each year the city celebrated a magnificent festival in honor of the "Divine Meeting," with statues of Mut and Amun uniting for a visit, of course, each cruising independently in their sacred barques, along with Khons. The Thebans, royal and common, called Mut the "Great Mother" and "Maker of Sound Bodies"—an appeal to her midwifery skills. She was said to be "rich in magic" as well as a benefactress of procreative fertility. These, of course, were typical major-goddess duties.

Mut in Myth

Mythologically, Mut was not a terribly overactive goddess. Her priests, mindful of the demiurge privileges, claimed that she was a celestial force that, in Great Cow form, gave Amun a much-needed ride through the cosmos on his way to triumph at Thebes. This is interesting, but Mut's appearances at Heliopolis as a companion goddess and "Eye of Ra" are quite late in comparison to the Pyramid Texts. Moreover, the original "Great Cow" role belonged to other goddesses later absorbed in various ways by Mut, including Mehueret, Hathor, Hezat, Nut, and possibly even marginalized Amaunet. The association with Amon-Ra and absorption of Sekhmet made Mut very comfortable wherever any cult of Amun flourished in any of his forms, or wherever a lioness/cat-headed goddess was honored. For this reason, Mut was especially venerated at Bubastis, Memphis, and Hermonthis, as well as at numerous outlying oases. In return, the goddess shared *her* magnificent temple at Thebes with sister-goddesses like Sekhmet, Hathor, and Bastet.

One myth claims that Mother Mut was one of the deities who initially helped Isis collect the skin of the dismembered Osiris, but this appears to be an understandable attempt by her influential priesthood to attach their Queen to the increasingly popular Osirian family of gods in the late New Kingdom. In a further embellishment of that tradition, Mut appears alongside Nephthys in some texts as the chief wet-nurse of the infant Horus.

As stated, Mut's political powers were considerable, once her husband came to rule the spiritual and economic fortunes of the Two Lands. She was therefore obliged to steamroll goddesses in various locales at leisure. Knowing that her personality was associated at an early period with that of Nekhbet, it is not surprising to find that Mut's name is dropped frequently amid the scant ruins of the temple complex at El Kab. The cultic alliance with Amun could also be a mixed bag in some respects. Although it attained for Mut a national status she would never have achieved on her own, it also meant that her personality was completely overshadowed by that of her companion, even outside glorious Thebes. The positive aspect of this unavoidable subsidiary role was that Mut owned her own temples, chapels, shrines, and faithful devotees in just about every community built to honor her formidable partner. She was worshipped from Thebes to Medinet Habu to Tanis to Qasr Al-

Daklah. In some places, like Azbat Bashindi, she appears to be the chief object of temple-cult without overt local dependence upon Amun.

Throughout Greco-Roman times, Mut's worship proved durable at Thebes and a few of the Ptolemies added various shrines and gateways to her temple precinct at Asheru. Once joined to the temple of Amun-Ra by an extraordinary avenue lined with sphinxes, nothing but scattered remnants can be seen today. Known as "The Mistress of Asheru," Mut's sacred zone was built around a crescent-shaped lake hearkening to the northern shrine of Bastet, and was originally well-appointed by Pharaoh Amenophis III, who decorated the sanctuary with 574 black basalt statues of Mut's ominous alter ego, Sekhmet. Thereby he sought to endow her temple with more magical potency than belonged to any other goddess-sanctuary.

REMNANTS OF MUT: Though the majority of her Theban sanctuary and statuary has been destroyed and carted away by looters and other "collectors" over the centuries, many of the huge Sekhmet-of-Asheru images still sit, haunting and resplendent, amid the reeds and overgrown gullies that mark the utterly ruined parameters of Mut's temple. You'll also find them in museums ranging from Cairo to the Louvre in Paris, and even at the Vatican. That being noted, Mut's iconographic image appears throughout the Karnak and Luxor complexes and in scores of other temples in the wider region of Thebes and beyond. She's unmistakable, wearing her Double Crown—signifying the power of a goddess deemed fit to preside over the entirety of the Egyptian empire at an extraordinary point in time. Journeys to outlying shrines like Bashindi and Deir Al-Medineh are far less advisable without the assistance of a highly knowledgeable guide and a determination to hunt this great goddess down. A glimpse of Mut's still-haunting sacred "Lake of Asheru" in Thebes will prove satisfying, but don't wander off toward the precinct without permission: it may be off-limits due to ongoing excavation work.

Neith

Chief Role: Goddess of Creation, Patroness of Hunters and Weavers
Chief Title: "Mistress of the Bow"
Cult Centers: Sais, Esna, Memphis

Neith was mythical proof that at least one ancient Egyptian goddess could easily get away with doing what was allegedly a male god's work. While some goddesses might be whiling away the hours in figurative luxury, tending to the needs of their divine mates or offspring, Neith was out slinging arrows from her magical bow, brandishing her war shield, or bringing entire worlds into being! This goddess needed no male divinity to fight her battles or occupy her city. Rather, Neith was a goddess ahead of her time—perhaps too far ahead.

Mighty and majestic throughout ancient Egyptian history, Neith was old—perhaps the oldest primary goddess in the archaeological record. Certain funerary artifacts dating from Dynasty I point to the existence of her worship. Possibly originating in Libya, Neith's cult eventually centered in the Nile Delta, near the settlement of Sais. When the Delta came under Southern rule in Dynasty I, Neith's domain spread throughout the entire region of Lower Egypt. At this early stage in Egyptian history, tribal customs did not dictate that a goddess *must* be considered subsidiary to a male god. As a result, Neith never seems to have taken a submissive position to any male god within the confines of her own cult.

The Mightiest of Goddesses

Neith's ancient fetish and symbols were the hunting-bow and the war-shield. These motifs, along with the crossed bows that were the standard of her nome, indicate that her original followers considered her to be not only self-sufficient but somewhat androgynous. Neith's identity was so formidable that she was said to have formed the universe by herself, emerging fully-formed from the primordial waters of Chaos and fashioning both Earth and the Firmament with Seven Words or "Seven Shots" from her quiver of arrows. The priests at Sais were revered for their wisdom among all the priests of Egypt and they claimed that Neith brought the first gods into being as well. This quality of Neith as the demiurge may have been aptly reflected in one possible interpretation of her Egyptian name, meaning "That Which Exists."

So prominent was Neith in Lower Egypt that her cult ruled supreme there through much of the Old Kingdom Period. She stood as the primary protectress of the Delta and from at least Dynasty V wore the Red Crown to prove it. Some scholars believe the Red Crown of Lower Egypt may have been an actual embodiment of her aforementioned ancient name, rendered *nj.t* in English transliteration of the phonetic value of the hieroglyphs.

The Wisest Goddess

When it came to dispensing wise advice, Neith was considered the ultimate source by mortals and gods alike. A late version of the Horus myth relates that she was consulted by letter when the tribunal of gods was bickering over whose side to take in the Horus-Set contentions. Though reticent to testify in person, Neith sent a letter back to the tribunal in favor of Horus, threatening to make the sky fall down upon all the gods if her will was ignored. Neith's powers over the cosmos were well-established by virtue of her early role in creation and further fostered by her assimilation of Mehueret, the great cosmic

Flood-Cow. As the reader noted in the Isis article, most of the gods were fearful of Neith's threat, with the conspicuous exception of Ra. Ra was indeed unafraid, a fact that may be a mythical nod to the historical usurpation of Neith's creative priorities by Atum-Ra in Egyptian cosmology. Perhaps in retort, Neith was sometimes given the title "Mother of Ra," as if to remind everyone of *her* original cosmic seniority.

In addition to her generative talents, Neith incorporated other attributes, especially in the funerary realm. She acted as one of the protectresses of the sacred "Canopic Jars" containing the embalmed organs of the deceased, along with the other three defenders of the dead: Isis, Nephthys, and Serqet. In this capacity, Neith was the guardian of the stomach and that organ's jackal-headed *genie* "patron," Duamutef.

A possible confusion of Neith's trademark crossbow with the image of a weaving-woman's shuttle may have led to her role as a patroness of those who operated the loom. The Egyptians were famous for their fine linen (even in ancient times), so this was no small endorsement for the goddess. Inevitably, this particular identity led back to the funerary scene and a cameo appearance for Neith as a weaver of the Osirian burial garments. This role was usually fulfilled by Isis and Nephthys, or by variant "Shentayit" forms of those two goddesses. Neith's inclusion in such mythological cycles and in the mortuary tradition as a whole was no doubt facilitated by the presence of her cult alongside that of Osiris in the Delta region. As the Osirian family rose to greater prominence after Dynasty XII, priests of Neith must have sought to associate their goddess with the burgeoning cult.

The Decline and Restoration of Neith

Neith's early role as sole *creatrix* was most clearly snubbed by the powerful theologians at Heliopolis and Memphis, who sought to attribute these powers to their own chief gods, Atum-Ra and Ptah. Even so, Neith's importance and antiquity could not be easily swept aside. With the continued rise of the solar cult after Dynasty V, and the Osirian cult after that, Neith's cult did experience centuries of gradual national decline. Hathor and Sekhmet (with whom she was often associated) could appear just as powerful in their own fashion and soon Neith was no longer alone in her stance as a distinctly mighty, independent goddess. Moreover, Hathor and Skehmet, for all their powers, were willing to assume roles as the consorts of equally powerful male deities. Neith occasionally paired with Sobek.

It is also interesting that it was Wadjet, mighty cobra goddess of Buto, who primarily held fast to the official limelight as tutelary patroness of Lower Egypt. Even though Neith was likely the first to wear the Red Crown of Lower Egypt, Wadjet came to be the typical representative. There can be no doubt that the two goddesses were very closely linked in their

Delta domains, for in the pre-Dynastic period their neighboring cities were successive capitals for the "Hornet Kings." For this reason, we must entertain at least the possibility that Neith and Wadjet were the same goddess in two different, localized forms, with a delta *uraeus* goddess named Mehyt perhaps serving as a syncretistic bridge between the two. Even in the New Kingdom, Neith's emblem could be found emblazoned upon Pharaoh's own Wadjet *uraeus* crown as a means of fortifying the protective magical powers associated with the symbol. This seems to be another strong indication of the residual identities shared by the two goddesses, ostensibly due to their geographical proximity.

Neith's cult experienced its last revival when Saite nobles wrestled control of Lower Egypt from Dynasty XXV Nubian Kings. When this line of rulers came to power in 633 BCE they made Sais their capital and lavished new prestige upon its goddess, whom they affectionately called "Mother." Marked by an orientation to all things artful, the Saite Dynasty of kings lasted for over one hundred years until 525 BCE and the Persian Conquest. Neith lost a great deal of her official prominence in the years that followed, as slovenly minions of the ruler Cambyses damaged her spectacular temple and used it as a military garrison.

Assimilated By Isis

Once the Persian squatters were ousted from the precinct by Ptolemaic times and a measure of Neith's clout was restored, the goddess found her chief importance through absorption by Isis. The two goddesses had been Delta neighbors and rivals for centuries, with Isis the chief goddess at Busiris (and perhaps also at Behbeit). In Greco-Roman times, Neith was perceived as yet another "form" of popular Isis. Her annual celebration at Sais—the Festival of the Lamps—reflected this assimilation. This solemn, deeply spiritual occasion was closely connected with the Osirian mysteries at Busiris and the related Sokar Festival at Memphis—rites also involving the ferocious Sekhmet. The temple of Neith at Sais eventually became more renowned as a repository for Osirian relics and as the scene of Osirian ministrations than for its worship of the once-supreme demiurge.

Neith still retained her ancient reputation for wisdom, however. The Greek historian Herodotus implied that, in the 5th century BCE, Neith's temple was the site of a highly respected oracle. Such oracles were often a wise means for fading goddesses to maintain proper levels of prestige. As proof of her clout, Neith also possessed a famed temple at Memphis, in the cult-center of the god Ptah.

Chief Goddess of Esna

Though Neith was most associated with the Nile Delta, she *did* make inroads throughout Egypt during the course of her career. As noted, a famous temple of Neith was built just outside the walls of the city of Memphis, where the goddess was identified with Sekhmet and, as a “companion” goddess of ram-headed Khnum, Neith shared the fine temple in the Upper Egyptian city of Esna. This late, largely Roman-enhanced sanctuary was built for Khnum and Neith in their respective roles as creative divinities. How such geographically opposed immortals came together is still not entirely clear.

One may posit that rulers of the Saite Dynasty perhaps controlled substantial land-holdings near Esna, prompting them to establish a stronghold of the Neith-cult in that region at an earlier period. While this is speculative, there can be no question that the temple at Esna provides us with most of our information regarding the cosmic and mythical importance of Neith. The inscriptions at Esna speak of her in her original persona as the primordial goddess who initiated the universal creation process on her loom, swam downriver to her city of Sais for a little “rest,” and left Khnum in charge of finishing the job on his potter’s wheel.

Though Neith shared the temple at Esna with Khnum, she was not considered to be the consort of that god. True to her androgynous nature, Neith always seems to have remained a solitary goddess. Though dynastic sources (including a few spells in the Pyramid Texts) speak vaguely of Neith as a possible consort of the brutal Set—and as mother of the crocodile-god, Sobek, who was the ostensible fruit of that union—this association was not permanent or necessarily widespread. Neith’s relationship with Sobek was due far more to their cultic proximity in the "Crossed Bows" nome and later in the Fayyum Oasis region. In any case, Neith is occasionally depicted in the presumably painful act of suckling a baby crocodile—further proof of her mettle.

Neith's "motherhood" of Sobek, however, seems to be a contradiction to much more widespread legends which touted her as a celibate virgin-goddess along the lines of Artemis or Athena, with whom the Greeks quickly identified her. For this reason, Neith was readily equated with the *Lates* fish—a species of Nile perch occurring at Esna and reputed to have self-impregnating powers.

REMNANTS OF NEITH: Nothing but rubble is left to remind us of the once huge and majestic temple of Neith at Sais. Various blocks and scattered stones remain near the modern Delta site of Sa el-Hagar. There is, however, an interesting Dynasty XXX stele on display in the Cairo Museum that records how the temple of Neith at Sais once collected a tenth of all imported goods entering Egypt by way of Naukratis—not a bad percentage. Her temple at Memphis is long gone as well and there are few remnants of her days of glory in the Fayyum; there she was eclipsed by Isis-Renenutet. As it stands today, Neith's only extant sanctuary is the rather late but textually important Roman Temple at Esna.

Nekhbet

Chief Role: Patroness of Upper Egypt, Protectress of the King and Women in Childbirth
Chief Title: "Mistress of Nekheb" "The Great White One"
Cult Centers: Nekheb

The worship of Nekhbet may have lost some of its importance in the very latter days of Egyptian religion, but this vulture-headed goddess was one of the most powerful and important divinities in the Two Lands for a rather long time before her decline.

Starting out as a typical, local fetish-goddess, Nekhbet was intimately associated with *vulturamuas icidetis,* the Egyptian vulture. This motif was a feature of her iconography from the beginning. Nekhbet and her tribal followers were based in the settlement of Nekheb, which was close to the city of Nekhen (later called Hierakonopolis), a metropolis that rose to archaic prominence as the capital of the southern realm of Egypt. Horus was the great god of Nekhen and Nekhbet's proximity to his town did not hurt her status. In fact, friendly relations between the two communities allowed Nekhbet's town to acquire early control of key trade routes leading to the Red Sea and various Arabian mines. Basically, Nekhbet was a goddess in the right place at the right time.

When the Two Lands were relatively unified circa 3000 BCE, Nekhbet's cult rose to more than a local prominence and she was regarded as a symbolic protectress of all Upper Egypt and the pharaohs. Her attributes as a vulture made her a perfect guardian for the "White Crown" and she later managed to secure an occasional position as part of the royal headdress, next to the *uraeus* and her northern companion-goddess, Wadjet of Buto. The two goddesses appear to have gained their greatest national exposure by appearing in temple reliefs of Pharaoh, guarding his head with ferocious devotion, or in human form preparing to place the Double Crown upon his brow—a sure sign that his ascension to the throne was ratified by the tutelary goddesses of both "Realms."

Nekhbet, Consort of the Nile Inundation

Despite close quarters with Nekhen, Nekhbet was not widely considered the spouse of Horus. Rather, in the early-going, she was considered the consort of Hapy, the god who many mistakenly consider the personification of the Nile River. Hapy was, in fact, the embodiment of the annual Nile *flood* and its attendant fertility. Primitive images sometimes portray Nekhbet herself with the rounded belly characteristic of the androgynous Hapy. Pyramid Texts also speak of Nekhbet's ample breasts, another indication that she may have been, at the outset, a mere feminization of Hapy later assimilated to the vulture fetish.

As if to make Nekhbet's origins even more enigmatic, the Pyramid Texts speak of her as the "Great White Cow of Nekheb." Though this doesn't blend with the vulture persona, such bovine characteristics certainly helped Nekhbet when she fulfilled her mythical task of blocking the "Entrance of the Abyss"—an obscure cosmological role related most likely to the detention of the dreaded Apophis serpent, enemy of Order and symbol of Chaos. Nekhbet's guise as a cow-goddess also indicates her motherly nature and an early dynastic role as nursemaid for the infant pharaoh. This nursing attribute would remain a primary feature of her cult until the end.

In some ancient texts, Nekhbet plays a vague role in the actual birth of Osiris, but this likely stemmed from her long-standing reputation as a guardian of women in labor—a job almost *every* under-worked Egyptian goddess seems to have assumed to keep her cult functional. Nekhbet's special powers in the childbirth and nursing departments made her fervently sought-after by pregnant women and those who desired to conceive.

As a tutelary goddess always bound to her city and region, Nekhbet enjoyed a loyal following in Nekheb, where she came to actually absorb Hathor as a personality and where she owned a sizeable temple complex. Outside of Nekheb, however, she was a subsidiary goddess in various temples—her cult image receiving attention in special sanctuaries at Thebes, Memphis, and certainly at Hierakonopolis, where she was considered, in her Hathor-Nekhbet form, to be a companion of Horus. At Nekheb (modern El Kab), when her association with Hapy diminished, she was regarded alternately as a consort of Sobek or even as a spouse of the god Thoth. These goddesses got around. Nekhbet retained her measure of honor even into Ptolemaic and Roman times, when Eurgetes II and Soter II refurbished her shrines at Nekheb. The Greek rulers especially loved Nekhbet, identifying her with their own goddess of childbirth, Eileithyia.

REMNANTS OF NEKHBET: As a signature goddess of Egyptian royalty, the actual image of Nekhbet is one of the most ubiquitous in temple iconography. As part of the headgear of pharaohs, queens, and fellow goddesses, she can be seen in virtually every sanctuary and relief. In modern El Kab there can still be viewed several ruined shrines and chapels dedicated to the great vulture goddess, dating from numerous periods, and all testifying to the durability of her cult throughout the greater portion of ancient Egyptian history.

Nephthys

Chief Role: Goddess of Transitional Death, Protection, and Divine Assistance
Chief Title: "Sister of the God," "Mistress of the Mansion of the Sistrum"
Cult Centers: Diospolis Parva, Komir, Sepermeru

If you've ever been one of those persons with special talents and qualities, yet forced to live in the constant shadow of your flashier siblings, then you and the goddess Nephthys would have a lot to commiserate about. Nephthys has long remained one of the more elusive figures in the ancient pantheon, even though she achieved fame and fortune just for being a member of the Great Ennead of Heliopolis. Her ancient name, *Nbt Hwt,* pertains to the architecture of the temple precinct and literally means "Mistress of the Enclosure." It is really more of a descriptive title than a proper name.

It is likely that Nephthys began her career as a variant form of some *other* goddess, perhaps the architecturally inclined Seshat, with whom she is closely identified as early as the Dynasty V Pyramid Texts and throughout most of ancient Egytian history. As a goddess whose specialty was the protective embrace, Nephthys could also have been a local Heliopolitan deity whose purpose was to guard some aspect of the sacred dwelling, another role she would play at all junctures. The best guess may likewise be the simplest: Nephthys was *exactly* what her nickname seems to indicate—a divine personification of the embracing enclosure-wall that "protected" the ancient temple.

Whatever the case, we do know that Nephthys became one of the renowned goddesses of Egypt by at least Dynasty V. From the Pyramid Texts we learn that she was believed to be the last child born to Geb and Nut on the fifth intercalary day. The texts also imply that she was a companion, of some sort, to her brother, Set, but this was not as clearly delineated as the partnership of Isis and Osiris.

We learn instead that Nephthys was more suitably the inseparable companion and "shadow" of her sister, Isis, whom she joined as mourner and protector of the murdered Osiris.

Stalwart Companion of Isis

In the Pyramid Texts, Isis and Nephthys are depicted as ideal complementary companions, the two wailing-women whose tears (and magic) made it possible for Osiris to be resurrected. By association, this powerful pairing of the Two Sisters made it possible for the pharaoh to enter the afterlife under divine protection. While various strains of the later legend note that Nephthys's erstwhile spouse, Set, imprisoned the body of Osiris in a gilded chest and cast it into the Nile, the same strains of myth seem swift to indicate that Nephthys sided with Isis in her plight, joining her in a search for the lost king. Later, when Set ripped Osiris into pieces and scattered the body-parts across Egypt, Nephthys is again at her sister's side as a faithful helper. It is after the body of Osiris has been reconstituted that Nephthys fulfills her crucial mythical role.

The two grief-stricken sisters, uniting their powers, mourn until their cries pierce the heavens. Transforming themselves into kite-birds they fly in harrowing arcs among the treetops and, beating their wings, both are able to force the breath of new life into Osiris, helping to enact his resurrection and then steadfastly protecting his mummy. Thus they secure a place of glory for Osiris (and Pharaoh) in the underworld. This union of the Two Sisters in misery and magic was far more than a sentimental motif to strike the heart of the ancient Egyptian. Indeed, what these united goddesses did for the revivification and protection of the Osirian mummy preserved the balance of life, death, and renewal.

The benevolent acts of Isis and Nephthys guaranteed the entire welfare of Egypt and the power of these acts emanated from every royal/funerary and cult temple. It was crucial that Nephthys and Isis could accomplish for Pharaoh what they had wrought for Osiris. By virtue of these associations, Nephthys was therefore a goddess who could act protectively on behalf of every ancient Egyptian, in concert with Isis or sometimes even on her own. This magically charged function was intrinsic to the belief that the order of *ma'at* must be maintained for the benefit of the local temple, the royal throne, and the community. Nephthys was perhaps best known by epithets such as "The Excellent" and "Sister of the God," for it was she who completed the necessary power-equation with Isis and guarded the Osirian mummy in virtually every temple and locale. Neglect of this protective duty would conceivably result in the collapse of the world into chaos or disaster. Make no mistake about it: the Egyptian priests and people took the dual role of the Two Sisters very seriously.

Mother of Anubis?

According to mythological cycles that seem to have become conflated after the New Kingdom, Nephthys estranged herself from Set following the betrayal of Osiris. Some versions of lore indicate that, before this separation, a lonely Nephthys sought comfort in the arms of Osiris, disguising herself as Isis and weakening the god's powers of discernment. After the seduction, Nephthys became pregnant and hid herself away from everyone in the Delta marshlands. Upon giving birth to the dog-headed god, Anubis, Nephthys was so overwrought that she abandoned the child to the elements and wild beasts.

Isis, however, became aware of the dilemma; a pack of wild dogs that found the infant were in her service and they alerted their mistress. After rescuing Anubis, Isis took it upon herself to raise him in secret, teaching him great sorcery with the assurance that he would one day prove valuable to the kingdom. As for Nephthys, it was said that Isis loved her sister almost as much as she loved her husband. The two were bound by the strongest of ties. Through the mediation of Thoth, Isis forgave Nephthys for the adulterous episode and harmony was restored.

Perhaps returning the favor, Nephthys is often given the role of fostering the child Horus and nursing him at her breast, a job that would take on (or reflect) significant pharaonic priorities via identification of the king with the son of Isis and Osiris. Nephthys was the original "sister who keeps watch among the bulrushes."

Other Roles of Nephthys

In tandem with Isis, Nephthys also represented one of the majestic flagstaffs that adorned temple pylons and, perhaps by extension, the sisters personified the pylons themselves. This function could also be a derivative of Nephthys's more general core-identity as "Mistress of the Enclosure." As one who assimilated the personality of Seshat, Nephthys was also considered a patron of the temple library—the House of Life—and keeper of decrees and records in both earthly and heavenly spheres. Nephthys's personality truly seems to have been that of an all-purpose, faithful "divine assistant," and is perhaps best exemplified by her title, She-Who-Carries-Out-the-Orders-of-the-Gods.

Despite her constant loyalty to Isis and Osiris, Nephthys was probably also a rather macabre figure in the estimation of most Egyptians. Female children were rarely named after Nephthys, perhaps because it would not have made sense to associate a child with an epithet, much less one specifically denoting the temple or its guard-wall. Another reason, however, is likely due to the fact that Nephthys could be regarded as the darker side of Isis—a being that embodied the more ominous aspects of her sister's positive nature. Whereas the tears of Isis and Nephthys were often praised as dual sources of the annual inundation, Nephthys could likewise be worrisome because *her* tears were believed to accelerate the process of bodily decay and putrefaction. Though Nephthys was beloved by the Egyptians for her altruism, they may not have wished to name their daughters after a goddess linked to rotting flesh.

While Isis and Nephthys enjoyed a distinct primacy over certain funerary themes, Isis represented that aspect which resulted in blissful new existence and rejuvenation, whether in the hereafter or in the blessed event of childbirth. Nephthys, on the other hand, was seen as the unpleasant (but necessary) personification of that transition through which the dead *must* pass before entering eternity. One of her most intriguing titles is "Sovereign of the Embalmer's Workshop," which was accorded to her at Memphis and hearkens to these morbid themes. This was apparently an early motif in regard to Nephthys, for the Pyramid Texts mention the struggle of Pharaoh to break free from the "tresses of Nephthys," which were considered one and the same with the linens used in mummification. In the same text, however, Pharaoh is assured that the tresses of Nephthys are *not* bonds; they seem instead to serve a protective, nurturing purpose almost akin to that of the chrysalis or the cocoon.

In purely cosmic terms, Nephthys represented the twilight and rode the Solar Bark of Ra that drifted into coming darkness, whereas Isis represented the same bark entering the new dawn. Another ancient and obscure epithet of Nephthys was "She Who Fashions the Body of the Gods," which again seems to pertain to her overall role as some sort of helpful divine organizer working on behalf of the entire pantheon. With Isis, however, Nephthys sits prominently in the tribunal that ratifies the "Weighing of the Heart" at Final Judgment. When the deceased soul came to the very end of its journey before the fearsome Osiris, it was Nephthys who joined Isis with fortifying arms upheld behind the throne of their lord and king.

Nephthys was assigned guardianship of the sarcophagus and normally (though not always) depicted at the head of the coffin for protective purposes, while Isis was positioned at the feet. In similar capacity, Nephthys was the defender of the Canopic Jar containing the lungs of the embalmed, acting as patroness of the *genie* Hapi. The Egyptians also believed that, as a powerful sorceress in her own right, Nephthys could protect the living or dead with her spells. The abundance of ancient *faience* amulets of Nephthys (and even spells invoking her) indicates that the common folk were rather inclined to invoke this divinity. As the constant and efficient companion of the wildly popular Isis, we should not be surprised to learn that a great deal of the proverbial limelight spilled onto Nephthys. She had her own followers.

At funerals, perhaps as early as the Middle Kingdom, two female family members seem to have been selected to represent Isis and Nephthys in the act of wailing for the deceased. Likewise, at later festivals and celebrations of the Osirian Mysteries, Nephthys occupied a role, particularly in December, when the "Lamentations of Isis and Nephthys" were dramatically reenacted by two virgin-priestesses over a three-day period. During the associated Khoiak Festival, Nephthys took her place with over thirty other divinities in her own bark-shrine, floating on the candlelit waters of any given temple's sacred lake.

Though positive transition and goodly protection constituted the domain of Nephthys, she remained essentially a mirror-image of—and counterpoint to—her sister. Still, her contribution was indispensable. For example, Isis would rarely be portrayed enacting the specific temple rites of Osirian protection and revivification without Nephthys and *vice versa.* In virtually every major sanctuary, Nephthys was stationed with Isis to protect the local "relic" of Osiris. Like her sister, however, Nephthys possessed a flexible nature and was not always so shadowy. For example, Nephthys could often appear as a fire-breathing goddess of raging power in her efforts to protect the Osirian mummy at various temples. One of her epithets at the temple of Horus at Edfu was Merkhetes, or "She Who Sears with Flame." In this capacity, Nephthys is an actively aggressive goddess associated with Sekhmet and Mehyt. Within such cultic contexts, her anger could be appeased only by meat offerings or the rattling of the sistrum.

Though one quaint myth portrays Nephthys as an accessory to childbirth (see the Meskhenet article), she was never really a deity of home and hearth. Contrary to some beliefs, Nephthys's name (often misconstrued as "Lady of the [domestic] House") had nothing to do with the common Egyptian housewife. There is some indication that her name *could* be used as a pun to represent the wives/helpmates of priests or other female caretakers of the temple precinct, but this association is late, ephemeral, and perhaps too opportunistic to indicate any value in determining original meaning.

However, when the Nile flood was so abundant that it touched the outskirts of the wastelands and caused new life to bloom, this phenomenon was apparently believed (in late times) to represent some fertile, reproductive aspect of Nephthys. The idea is clearly a corollary of the mythical tryst with Osiris. Though hailed as wet-nurse of Horus and the pharaohs, her maternal qualities were nevertheless suspect in most places, despite this late belief that she conceived Anubis. As if to caution us against placing too many restrictions on Nephthys's personality, there is at least one Ramesside-era reference to her being the mother of a daughter with the warrior-god, Hemen, of the town of Mo'Alla.

Nephthys's generally childless nature is perhaps best implied in the Pyramid Texts via a spell in which the pharaoh is encouraged to "make fun" of the great gods who have assisted him, lest they somehow turn against his interests. He is urged to accomplish this by calling various gods insulting names that highly exaggerate some of their perceived shortcomings. Hence, kindly Isis is ridiculed with the name "Putrid Crotch," while Nephthys is called "Substitute Woman with No Vagina." Osiris, Thoth, and Horus are likewise insulted in this strange passage and, needless to say, these grand gods were never addressed in such a manner under typical circumstances.

Cults of Nephthys

Though her personality is far less-definitive when compared with that of Isis, Nephthys was still a goddess of considerable prestige. Ramesses II himself built a temple for her in the frontier-town of Sepermeru, midway between Oxyrhynchus and Herakleopolis, in what was once Upper Egyptian Nome XIX. There, alongside temples of Set and Ra-Harakhte, her sanctuary was called "The House of Nephthys of Ramesses-Meriamun," and was specifically endowed with pharaonic land-holdings under the administration of her prophets and *wab* priests. According to Papyrus Wilbour, another temple (also dubbed The House of Nephthys of Ramesses-Meriamun) appears to have been built in affiliation with Set and Ra-Harakhte institutions in Su, nearer to the Fayyum Oasis.

These special foundations indicate a well-known reverence of the Ramesses kings for Set's coterie of gods, but also hint at a possibly unique link between the cults of Ra-Harakhte, Set, and Nephthys. Without question, it is quite important to remember that Nephthys remained the close associate of Set in many territories and shared with him a primacy over certain outlying portions of the kingdom. In such areas, Set was not considered the utterly evil god of Osirian legend, but rather as a valiant warrior who aided Ra by slaying the malevolent serpent, Apophis, during Ra's perilous journey in his Night Bark. We have already seen indications that Nephthys was the protective goddess of the Night Bark of Ra, so the presence of shrines dedicated to Sethian deities may have been especially pertinent in regions where the Ra-Apophis myth was prominent. Lending potential credence to this theory, we have the testimony of Papyrus Bologna, also from the Ramesside era. Therein, a prophet of Set named Pra'emhab invokes what appears to be the local triad of "Ra-Harakhte, Set, and Nephthys" and complains to an official that he is overworked and taxed beyond his duties at Set's "house" in the town of Punodjem:

"...I am responsible for the ship, and I am responsible likewise for the House of Nephthys and the heap of other temples to all the gods of the district."

From the Late Period through Greco-Roman times, prophets and various other cult personnel of Nephthys are attested for Antaeopolis, Heracleopolis, Saqqara, Heliopolis, Kom Ombo, and Diospolis Parva (Hwt-Sekhem). In the latter city, Nephthys was originally part of a family-cult consisting also of Osiris, Isis, and Horus. By Greco-Roman times, however, Nephthys achieved a special distinction because of some innovative tradition that she was literally "born" in the town, and that she gave unique protection to Osiris in his guise as the Bennu Bird—or Sacred Phoenix—under her form of Nephthys-Khereseket. Her late prominence at Diospolis Parva (or "Hwt") may have been due in large part to the fact that her name already meant "Mistress of [the] Hwt." At the same time, Nephthys had also become increasingly identified with Hathor as a goddess of beer, beauty, joy, and ribald celebration. Thus, just as Hathor had assimilated the town's earlier goddess, Bat, so Nephthys assimilated Hathor and their personalities become interchangeable at Diospolis Parva. Inscriptions in almost all of the contemporaneous Greco-Roman temples pointedly refer to Nephthys as the chief goddess of Upper Egyptian Nome VII. It became her special territory and she was known far and wide as "Mistress of the Mansion of the Sistrum."

Also from the Late Period through Greco-Roman times, there was a popular temple of Nephthys at Komir, about twelve kilometers from Esna. Here, Nephthys was called "Mistress of the District of the Gazelle" and shared her sacred estate with the goddess Anukis. Nephthys reigned at Komir because of her status as a primary protective goddess at an Osirian shrine to the north, in Esna, while Anukis reigned as a primary goddess of the First Cataract region in the south. Again, we witness dualities at work in ancient Egyptian cult. The temple was a key stop on the annual sojourn of Hathor's barge to Edfu for the Festival of Beautiful Meeting.

Otherwise, statue-cults of Nephthys were almost certainly maintained in many temples throughout Egypt, including Edfu, Busiris, Coptos, Medmaoud, Naqada, Thebes, Dendera, Philae, Behbeit, Mendes, etc. Her national birthday festival was the last epagomenal day on the Egyptian calendar and she was the object of an important local feast at Edfu called "The Heart of Nephthys Rejoices."

REMNANTS OF NEPHTHYS: Like her closest associates, this ubiquitous goddess can be found in virtually every extant temple and tomb across Egypt, particularly in tandem with

Isis. Look for her especially in the temples at Philae, Edfu, and Dendera, where she was one of the chief divinities in each local pantheon. Her temple at Komir has not been fully excavated and, though it features a beautiful hymn to Nephthys on the rear exterior wall, it is not at this time accessible to the average tourist.

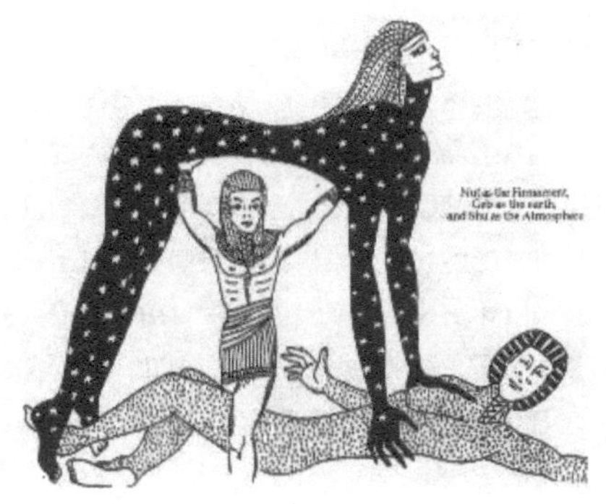

Nut

Chief Role: Goddess of the Firmament, Protectress of the Dead
Chief Title: "She Who Gives Birth to the Gods"
Cult Centers: Heliopolis

Like other deities before they were co-opted by the theologians of Heliopolis, Nut was probably a local goddess whose cult was tailored to meet the purposes of creationist mythology. Some scholars point to the possibility that Naunet of Hermopolis was, in fact, the original Nut. This is far from certain.

After Nut was given a place in Heliopolitan cosmology as the daughter of Shu (the Air) and Tefnut (Moisture), legend records that she simply tore her way out of her mother's womb, a favor that would later be repaid by one of her own offspring. Appearing in the Dynasty V Pyramid Texts, Nut was portrayed as consummating an incestuous love-affair with her brother, Geb, the god of the vegetative earth. Other versions of the myth make matters even more sordid, revealing that Nut's father, Shu, harbored a secret lust for his daughter. One day he happened to catch his offspring in the throes of passion and got between them to literally pry them apart. To maintain their separation, Shu lifted Nut so high above Geb that she became the very Firmament itself.

Obviously, this was how the separation of Earth and Sky was believed to occur in ancient Egyptian (Heliopolitan) thought. Nut remained in her lofty position and only her hands and feet were able to touch the earth, resting on the peaks of Bakhu and Manu, the Mountains of Sunrise and Sunset.

The Offspring of Nut

Though Shu had been successful in separating Geb and Nut, the goddess had already become pregnant. The first coupling was significant, for Nut gave birth to an enormous brood—the stars, planets, and all of the other cosmic bodies. These countless, sparkling children did not stray far from their mother, opting to remain fixed to her vast belly, giving the heavens their shimmering light. This is one reason why Nut was often depicted in reliefs and paintings as a woman stretched across the sky with a star-studded abdomen. Even so, Nut's fecundity angered her lustful father, Shu.

In addition to holding her aloft by day and by night, he conferred with Ra, the solar disc, and pronounced a curse upon his daughter, decreeing that she should never bear another child on any day of the year. In effect, she was cursed across the calendar!

Nut, however, was a wily and patient goddess. To satisfy her needs, it is said that she seduced Thoth, the god of wisdom and time. In a game of dice, the crafty Nut won five "secret" days from the powerful deity—five days *not* featured on the 360 day calendar. Seeing a potential loophole in her father's curse, Nut made good use of those extra "epagomenal" days. She gave birth to five children, all of them destined for fame and (mis)fortune:

Day 1—Osiris
Day 2—Haroeris
Day 3—Set
Day 4—Isis
Day 5—Nephthys

To our modern sensibilities, the story of Nut seems fraught with dysfunction, but for the ancient Egyptians her saga captured a number of interesting perceptions about the physical world.

First, it dramatized the perception that the heavens and the atmosphere were not exactly one and the same in substance and that the latter—though invisible—separated the former from the earth. In a similar fashion, Nut was the Great Mother of the universe and the all-encompassing force that surrounded the world and prevented the frightening outer forces of Chaos from dashing down upon humanity in a wave of destruction. Nut's sly way of getting around her father's curse also explained why the ancient Egyptians added five intercalary days to the calendar year, seeking to harmonize solar and lunar time-frames. In the beginning, Nut was probably a goddess of the daytime sky and could be envisioned in bovine and anthropomorphic form. With the rise of the Heliopolitan cosmology, however, her domain was extended to all realms of the Firmament.

Nut maintained her distinction even after the birth of her infamous brood, all of whom became beings of the mortal sphere. The outsmarted Shu may have modified his original curse as well, for one strain of legend tells us that Nut would indeed go on to give birth each day. In this fashion, she swallowed the sun god in his form of Ra-Atum at sunset and then gave birth to him at dawn in his scarab-form of Khephri.

Being a celestial goddess may have hindered Nut's accessibility in terms of popular worship, but she was often invoked—with obvious good reason—as a mother-goddess. Meanwhile, her frequent appearance in cow-form identified her with deities like Hathor and Hesat. Even in the Pyramid Texts, Nut is envisioned as a refuge for Pharaoh after his death. As a result of this (and her subsequent identification with Hathor-Amentet), Nut became a ubiquitous funerary goddess. As protectress of the Theban necropolis and mourner for Pharaoh in the guise of her own son, Osiris, Nut would figuratively wail about the days when he was suckling happily at her breasts. She became *the* personification of the interior lid of the sarcophagus, where her protective, winged image was usually emblazoned. For king and citizen alike, the journey of death brought the departed soul into the receptive arms of this most universal of mothers.

The Worship of Nut

There is some evidence that, for a time, Nut was worshipped as a healing goddess in a special temple precinct in Memphis. Here she was evidently honored with a small temple of her own called "Pr-Nwt" or the "House of Nut." In this city, the sacred Sycamore tree was considered the dwelling place of both Nut and Hathor. From its branches, Nut (or Hathor) was believed to feed the deceased soul with all good things, thereby assuring the soul that its needs would be met in the afterlife. Nut's place in the Sycamore tradition seems to have been diminished in later times by the dominant presence of Hathor.

Dendera was another place where both Hathor and Nut were associated, particularly in the Greco-Roman era. In Hathor's chief city, appreciation of the firmament-goddess was reflected throughout the grand temple and especially in the glorious "New Year Chapel." Nut's image on the ceiling beguiled onlookers for centuries before removal for preservation at the Louvre museum. Nut also appears in the tiny "Temple of the Birth of Isis" situated directly behind the main temple of Hathor at Dendera. There, texts relate how Nut delivered Isis at Dendara under the watchful eye of Hathor, and later traipsed to Diospolis Parva to bring forth Nephthys. Nut's chief cult center, however, remained her own birthplace in Heliopolis, where she was honored with a sanctuary and a priesthood of her very own.

REMNANTS OF NUT: Marvelous ceiling inscriptions and reliefs at Dendara and Philae depict Nut in all her grandeur. Ask your guide to point out these astronomical masterpieces if you visit the temples. At the Cairo Museum, one peek inside the lid of most any sarcophagus will reveal the beautiful figure and loving face of Nut, who was the protectress of that portion of the coffin throughout much of ancient Egyptian history.

Renenutet

Chief Role: Royal Midwife, Nurse and Goddess of the Harvest
Chief Title: "Mistress of the Threshing Floor"
Cult Centers: Medinet Madi (Fayyum Oasis)

While the cobra-headed goddess Renenutet did not possess the royal prestige of a similar goddess like Wadjet, she did seem to enjoy greater popularity among the everyday Egyptians, particularly the agricultural laborers. Reverence for this goddess was at its strongest among farmers who routinely came across cobras hiding in their fields at harvest. Thus, these workers forever associated the cobra with that most bountiful time of the year. Renenutet, as their patron, was so powerful that her stare was said to make foes tremble—much the way the stare of any cobra in defense-mode might bother an unexpected interloper. Farmers in ancient Egypt believed that it was Renenutet who could coax a bountiful crop from the earth with that same mesmerizing gaze.

The Pharaonic Protectress

Renenutet makes several cameo appearances in the Pyramid Texts, acting as a protectress of Pharaoh in some auxiliary fashion with Wadjet; indeed, their association led to other pharaonic duties for the serpentine harvest-deity. In one tradition, Renenutet was considered to be the specific guardian of the pharaoh's linen wardrobe. At Thebes, she was linked with fellow cobra-goddess Mertseger, as well. Images of the two of them turn up in a number of royal tombs.

Owing to this funerary activity and an associated role as divine midwife, Renenutet also appears in some vignettes of the *Book of the Dead,* standing alongside Meskhenet in the Hall of the Two Truths. The deceased was said to rely upon these goddesses to "deliver" them as successfully into the afterlife as they could preside over the birth of newborns in the realm of the living.

As stated, the fearsome venom of the cobra did not prevent ancient Egyptians from cherishing Renenutet. This goddess retained her popular niche in matters of midwifery and, like Meskhenet, in establishing the destiny of newborns. The ancient meaning of her name is possibly related to or derived from such tasks. In the New Kingdom, she proved important in many localities for she was said to be as capable of guarding the granaries and fields as she was at securing good fortune for infants. Her festivals were held in late winter and early summer and were appropriately joyful events, marked by the offering of open-air sacrifices.

Renenutet's legendary value is sparse; she was sometimes known to be the mother of Nepri, a god of cornfields who was similar to Osiris in many respects. From at least Dynasty XII into Ptolemaic times, she had a detectable cultic association with the crocodilian god, Sobek. This union is evidenced by Renenutet's enormous popularity in the lush Fayyum region where she owned a number of sanctuaries, many of them alongside the temples of Sobek.

Isis, so very adept at convincing lesser Egyptian goddesses to share their attributes with her, gave Renenutet's Fayyum-cult its most significant "advance" by literally merging with her in the Late Period. This Isis-Renenutet fusion was honored under the Greek appellation "Isermouthis" and, in this guise, the cobra goddess enjoyed widespread worship in the Fayyum well into the Roman occupation and beyond.

REMNANTS OF RENENUTET: The ancient community of Darmouthis was sacred to

Renenutet, particularly under the Ptolemies. We have already noted her ubiquitous presence throughout the Fayyum. In the vicinity of the famed oasis, a number of extant monuments remind us of Renenutet's stature. For example, a first-century CE shrine (and altar) of Renenutet can still be found within the ruins of a temple of Sobek near the site of ancient Crocodilopolis. In Medinet Madi, a desert region just a few miles southwest of Fayyum City, one can visit the ruins of a tiny Dynasty XII temple dedicated to *both* Sobek and Renenutet.

In her form of "Isermouthis," Renenutet received an honorary cult at Dendara, where her image is found frequently throughout the temple of Hathor. She was likewise honored with statue-cults at Edfu, Thebes, and Kom Ombo, further demonstrating her popularity even in the latter days of ancient Egyptian religion.

Satis and Anukis

Chief Roles: Goddesses of the Inundation
Chief Titles: "The Voice of the Nile" (Satis), "She Who Embraces" (Anukis)
Cult Centers: Elephantine, Edfu (Satis), Sehel, Komir (Anukis)

At the outset, neither of these significant goddesses likely had anything to do with the ram-headed inundation god, Khnum. What they *did* possess was an enormous amount of power over the fertile aspects of the annual flood. Of the two, Satis appears to be the most ancient divinity. Her name is dropped a number of times in the Pyramid Texts, but her presence is possibly attested all the way back to Dynasty II. The holy island of Elephantine was likely her sole domain long before it became the fiefdom of Khnum.

In the Pyramid Texts, Satis and her water-pots serve some form of purification role for the deceased pharaoh. Early on, she appears to have been equated with Sothis, the personification of the Dog-Star—an annual harbinger of the coming flood. Anukis, it seems, emerged either from Sudan to the immediate south of the First Cataract region or from the north in a region perhaps between Esna and El Kab.

In the earliest Dynasties, both goddesses became entrenched in the First Cataract area near Elephantine, with Anukis settling on the lonely island of Sehel. They were not related divinities but considered as respective guardians of the official Egyptian frontier and manipulators of the inundation. Such powers made Satis and Anukis very popular with the farming classes around ancient Syene (Aswan).

Though they may have been rival goddesses at the outset, occupying rival islands, the rise of the cult of Khnum, the chieftain god of the extensive nome whose capital was Esna, eventually brought them together. First, Khnum and his powerful priesthood occupied

Elephantine Island and relegated Satis to a role as "consort." Only in the New Kingdom Period was Anukis forced into the equation as a second consort or even as a daughter of Khnum and Satis.

The Feral Goddesses

In early traditions, Satis displayed many of the same independent, warrior-like qualities attributed to the goddess Neith. Though she wore the White Crown of Upper Egypt, surrounded by the horns of the antelope, she carried a fearsome bow and arrow at her side. Her name seems to have meant "The Thrower" or "The Shooter," and due to her antiquity, this may indicate that she was regarded as a figurative "smiter" of Pharaoh's enemies or even as a goddess of the successful hunt. This last function is bolstered by the hieroglyph for her name, which appears to be an animal-skin skewered by an arrow.

The relationship between Satis and the flood cannot be underestimated, at least around

Elephantine Island. There, her little temple was built directly over a natural underground cavern or shaft in the rock, from which emanated the "Voice of the Nile." The gurgling noises made by rising flood waters at the bottom of this sluice supposedly alerted her priests (and thus the populace) to the coming inundation and even to its possible magnitude. For this reason, the flood was believed to actually emanate *from* Elephantine, and Satis maintained a unique association with the divination of the inundation even after Khnum had usurped her primacy. She was also a popular local goddess at Edfu, where a votive shrine appears to have been built for her in the main temple.

Anukis became a perfect companion for Satis in the New Kingdom because her name means "She Who Embraces" or "She Who Strangles," depending upon the interpretation. The role as embracer is thought to represent the manner in which Anukis, as Mistress of the Flood, "embraced" the appointed farmlands along the Nile without over-saturating them. Additionally, Anukis secured an alluring niche as a goddess of revelry and orgiastic abandon. In the Late Period, her followers were known to participate in licentious celebrations. Anukis was also closely associated with the gazelle in her temple at Komir to the north of Elephantine, although the parrot is sometimes related to her exotic persona.

Assimilated to Isis and Nephthys

Toward the end of the New Kingdom period, Satis and Anukis were known throughout Egypt, were the unrivaled goddesses of the First Cataract region, and were extremely popular across Lower Nubia as well. When the Osirian cult ascended, however, the entire triad of Khnum, Satis and Anukis was assimilated, to a certain extent. The Egyptians found it quite easy to see the threesome as yet another local manifestation of Osiris, Isis, and Nephthys. With the onset of the Late Period and the immense building projects at neighboring Philae and Bigeh, Isis was intimately identified with Satis, particularly in the guise of Sothis, while Nephthys came to own the temple at Komir with Anukis altogether.

REMNANTS OF SATIS AND ANUKIS: Satis owned a number of shrines on Elephantine Island, all of which were renovated or refurbished over the centuries. One elegant extant version has recently been reconstructed by a team of German archaeologists and appears to date from the reign of the glorious Hatshepsut herself. Visit the island on a day-trip from Aswan (with a knowledgeable guide) and marvel at the stylistic beauty and simplicity of this little temple to a grand goddess. There are also ruins of a temple originally dedicated to Horus and Satis at Al-Derr in Nubia, but Satis was ousted by the figure of Amun in the Middle Kingdom. The nerve! Far more scant are the ruins of the Anukis temple on the island of Sehel, although the two ladies are widely attested in that island's famous graffiti. Both also figure prominently in extant temple sites from Lower Nubia.

Despite the association between Khnum and Satis on Elephantine, the Roman-era temple of Khnum at Esna does not feature the goddess in significant fashion. There, Neith and a bevy of leonine goddesses form the requisite companions. Anukis is featured in a few prominent reliefs in the *pronaos,* however, alongside her alter ego Nephthys—a nod to their venerable cults at nearby Komir.

Sekhmet

Chief Role: Goddess of War, Plague, and Healing
Chief Title: "The Powerful One"
Cult Centers: Memphis, Imaou, Thebes

The ancient Egyptians had an immense amount of respect for the magnificent lions that haunted the outskirts of their civilization. In Western culture, it is customary to speak of the lion as the King of the Beasts, but it was not necessarily so with the Egyptians. Though male deities like Nefertum, Mihos, Aker, and Shu could take on impressive leonine form, the ancient Egyptians *best* deified these ferocious cats in the form of their goddesses.

Sekhmet was the most prominent of these lion-headed deities. Her cult is difficult to trace; one would think it had its origin in the desert places, on the outskirts, where lions might sneak like tawny nightmares to steal away livestock or the occasional, unwary human. Like her alter ego, Bastet, Sekhmet was originally a personification of the sun's more oppressive, unwelcome power. It is possible that the two ladies evolved from a common ancestral deity, but in the first dynasties, Sekhmet appears at Memphis and its Saqqaran environs. It is not clear if her cult was established there before that of her customary consort, Ptah. Even so, Sekhmet became the most prominent goddess in the district and apparently the most available, ending up as a companion to Sokar as well as to the cerebral Ptah. The latter of the two unions appears to have been the most durable and the twosome eventually "adopted" an obscure solar deity, Nefertum, as their son in the requisite triad.

Most Fearsome Goddess

As a warrior-goddess, Sekhmet was particularly irresistible to the pharaohs of the New Kingdom, where her figurative power was seen as a reflection of their own skill and ferocity on the battlefield. Sekhmet's role as the Eye of Ra, the Destroyer Sun, offered Kings like Ramses II the motif of a monstrous, fire-breathing lioness ready to burn all foes to cinder. No matter what the conquest, Sekhmet could provide assistance and victory, earning for herself such dainty titles as "Lady of the Messengers of Death," and "Smiter of Nubians."

When Sekhmet made her way into legend, it was at an early time and with a most virulent charge. In this manner she was viewed as the antithesis of the celebratory Hathor in raging form, when Ra sulked about being neglected by the people. To punish them, he sent his terrible Eye on a bloody rampage. Thus, Hathor and Sekhmet were opposite dimensions of the same goddess—one approachable and joyous, the other distant and full of vengeance. Likewise, they represented different aspects of the annual flood, with Sekhmet personifying the inundation when it was clearly out of control. One account of the legend, found in the tomb of Seti I, describes Sekhmet as the "Uncontrollable One" and she herself confesses that the blood of her victims is literally a balm for her very soul.

The Restorative Goddess

While it might be thought that such a violent goddess would be extremely unpopular, this was not at all the case with Sekhmet. Her cult was strong throughout the length and breadth of Egypt. The association with Hathor certainly helped, but Sekhmet's influential priesthood came up with another way to give her a tender, beneficial side—one that countered her more aggressive attributes.

When the inundation flowed each year from the distant mountains of central Africa, it often brought with it bacterium that could afflict the Egyptians with plague and various forms of parasitic disease. As Sekhmet was said to be the embodiment of a particularly raging flood, she was likewise said to possess a gift for curing every kind of disease its annual appearance seemed to "bring" to civilization. For this reason, Sekhmet's prophets were renowned as consummate healers, exorcists, and even veterinarians. Egyptians were convinced that Sekhmet's formidable power against the enemies of Ra and the pharaohs could be likewise utilized against affliction. Prophets of Sekhmet recited spells over sick individuals and their remedies were prized throughout the Two Lands.

Despite her healing nature, Sekhmet never relinquished her purely terrible qualities. According to one tradition, the last five days of the year (the intercalary days) were under her dominion and, especially during this time, she could wreak as much havoc and destruction upon humanity as she desired. To avoid calamity, the Egyptian priests in virtually every temple eventually took up "appeasement collections" and recited litanies of magical spells to soothe the wrath of the goddess. In truth, the attributes of this fascinating divinity may have embodied the realities of ancient existence more accurately than those of any other. Like life itself, Sekhmet could be harsh and randomly cruel, but also restorative…under the right circumstances.

At Memphis, Sekhmet is said to have possessed a temple of her own. Though Isis, Neith, and Hathor seem to have been equally popular in the city, Sekhmet maintained at least an honorary primacy up until the Late Period. Her cult was known in numerous other places, as well. For example, when Thebes had risen to supremacy and the prophets of the goddess Mut—along with the pharaohs—wished to expand the horizons of *that* particular goddess, they identified her with the Memphite Sekhmet. This was both a nod to Sekhmet's long-standing prestige and the need to assimilate her priorities. Long favored by pharaohs interested in expanding the empire through conquest, Sekhmet may well be considered part of the unique conglomerate—Mut-Sekhmet-Hathor—that represented *the* chief "composite-goddess" of Thebes. The Temple of Mut in the Asheru district of Thebes was as much the domain of Sekhmet as it was of Amun-Ra's great companion; hundreds of Sekhmet's images haunted the Mut temple-enclosure; there was *at least* one statue of Sekhmet for each day of the calendar year.

REMNANTS OF SEKHMET: While her temple at Memphis is probably lost forever, Sekhmet's identification with Hathor was honored with a sanctuary belonging equally to the two goddesses at Imaou, near the Delta region. It's not worth visiting (unless, perhaps, you happen to have specific business in

Imaou), but back in Thebes, numerous images of the enthroned Sekhmet still haunt the boggy precinct that houses scant ruins of Mut's Asheru temple-complex. Most of the legendary statues were long ago carted-away to foreign lands and museums like the Louvre and the Vatican Museum.

In the Karnak enclosure, the intrepid wanderer may inquire about the ruins of a small peripheral temple dedicated to Ptah and Sekhmet-Hathor. In this shrine lurks one of the most notorious little monuments in modern Egyptian archaeological lore—a statue of Sekhmet the Great. This particular image has struck a certain amount of fear into the hearts of local Egyptians (and tourists) for generations and has actually been held responsible for various cases of calamity and misfortune. What a thrill it would be to uncover the exact history of this image and how this statue of Sekhmet—among so many now scattered throughout the world—acquired its sinister reputation. Whatever the case, Sekhmet's prominence and enduring fame only goes to prove: you can't keep a *bad* goddess down.

Serqet

Chief Role: Protectress of the Dead and Afflicted
Chief Title: "Mistress of the Beautiful House"
Cult Centers: Edfu, Nome VI of Lower Egypt

It was inevitable that the scorpion would find an anthropomorphic representative in the seemingly endless pantheon of Egyptian deities; Serqet makes a most early debut on funerary stele dating from Dynasty I at Saqqara. Aside from any exposure gained by association with the now-legendary "Scorpion King," who appears to have existed during the Archaic Period, the desert-loving arachnids in question have always been prevalent throughout Egypt. People remain rather respectful of the scorpion's ability to inflict death or, at the very least, intense agony. On a more positive note, the ancient Egyptians believed that these creatures could serve in a defensive capacity, especially where Pharaoh was concerned. According to the Pyramid Texts, this is where Serqet makes an impact as fierce protectress of—you guessed it!—the king.

Associate of Mighty Isis

Like that of many other goddesses, Serqet saw her cult develop connections with the burgeoning Osirian family after Dynasty V. According to some versions of the developing legend, Serqet was one of the goddesses summoned to guard the infant Horus in the delta marshlands and keep him safe from the minions of Set. This makes sense because a temple complex, or a certain series of temples (called the "Mansions of Serqet"), probably existed in the delta region from early dynastic times. Scorpions were also part of the mythical entourage of Isis when that temporarily homeless goddess was drifting about from town to town, seeking shelter. On one such foray, Isis was accompanied by minions of Serqet with names like Tefen, Befen, Mestet, and, appropriately, *Pest*et. When one woman refused to give shelter to Isis, the scorpions promptly stung the woman's child. Of course, Isis came to the rescue with her magic and was rewarded with a roof over her head for at least one evening.

Serqet's own reputation for magical prowess made her quite an easy target for assimilation by Isis; with the onset of the New Kingdom, the two goddesses were often considered to be the same entity. In much earlier traditions, however, Serqet was thought to be one of the guardians of the four sources of the Nile flood and sometimes she appears as the caretaker of the hateful cosmic serpent, Apophis. Her potential role as a flood-goddess could hint at the origin of her name, which might be extrapolated to mean "She Who Opens [Cools] the Throat."

It should also be noted that this epithet could equally pertain to the effect of scorpion venom on the nervous system; respiratory failure and swelling of the throat were common symptoms of neurotoxic envenomation by several scorpion species. If Serqet was invoked against such envenomations (and there is evidence that her priests were skilled healers in this area) then this meaning of her name has special priority. Elsewhere, as part of the Osirian myth-cycle emanating from Heliopolis, Serqet secured a high-profile role as protectress of the dead. She guarded the Canopic Jar containing the intestines and was patroness of the attendant *genie* Quebesenuef. Though linked with the royal mortuary traditions throughout

Egypt, Serqet and her healing powers were a bit obscured by Isis in latter days.

REMNANTS OF SERQET: The independent cult of Serqet seems to have originated in Nome VI of the Delta region, based upon various archaeological attestations. As noted, priests of this goddess were known to have flourished in ancient Egypt. In later times, she appears to have been worshipped at Edfu, albeit along with many other deities. Her most famous archaeological legacy is the Amarna-style statue found guarding the Canopic Shrine in the tomb of Pharaoh Tutankhamun. Though it is a companion to equally graceful statues of Isis, Nephthys, and Neith, the image of Serqet has become one of the emblematic relics of the famous tomb. With her delicately splayed arms, nubile figure, and haunting expression, the Serqet statue is one of the world's most memorably exquisite works of ancient art. Be certain to get a glimpse of it at the Cairo Museum. For the extremely adventurous traveler, Serqet can be found as a prominent goddess in various Nubian temple ruins, though she appears to have possessed no sanctuary whatsoever in the ancient Nubian town the Greeks seemingly named after her—"Pselchis." Rather, she was the object of a cult as Isis-Serqet in the small but significant temple at Beit al-Wa'ali near Kalabsha.

Seshat

Chief Role: Record Keeper of Pharaoh's Achievements
Chief Title: "She Who Stretches the Cord"
Culter Centers: Hermopolis, Thebes

A variant of an ancient epithet of Seshat seems to be "She Who Lays Aside the Horns." Perhaps she did this in order to devote herself to the insurmountable task of eternal record-keeping. The long, reversed cow's horns atop Seshat's head appear often in her iconography, resting above what appears to be a multi-pointed star or blossom. Though somewhat akin to a divine accountant, Seshat was not exactly prim—she always wore a rather sensuous leopard-skin outfit to the "office."

Seshat was not one of the more accessibly popular goddesses of ancient Egypt, but she *was* one of the oldest and most important in terms of temple prestige. As early as Pharaoh Khasekhemwy in Dynasty II, she appears with her famous measuring-cord to help the king establish the parameters of the temple foundations (a *very* important ritual). As a later consort of the wise, ibis-headed god, Thoth, Seshat was believed to be the keeper of annals pertaining to all the rulers of Egypt. She was the goddess whose duty it was to record their accomplishments for the cosmic "log." The tools of her trade were the long, notched palm branch, a reed pen, and a palette.

As a matter of fact, Seshat was portrayed as recording *everything,* especially the plunder that warrior-kings accrued from conquered nations. In the eyes of the pharaohs, every captive—not to mention every goat, cow, or other form of captured livestock—had to be accounted for, and only a goddess like Seshat could keep up with the tally. She could even keep a detailed history of events and adventures experienced by those navigating the eternal journey of the afterlife.

Among builders and scribes, Seshat was a beloved patroness. Construction was Seshat's *forte* and she was always represented assisting the pharaoh at the initial founding of a temple. Here it is wise to remember that the building of every Egyptian temple was ideally the prerogative of Pharaoh *alone,* since he gave approval for the building, often provided the funds, and acted (at least figuratively) as the sole High Priest of whatever god or gods came to "dwell" within the sanctuary. Seshat held importance because she was said to supervise the painstaking ritual building-preparations in tandem with the king. Since Seshat was truly a mistress of the temple precinct or enclosure, it can be postulated that she was the original form of Nephthys, a goddess with whom she is closely associated as early as the Pyramid Texts, and by whom she was later usurped in some respects.

As noted, all generously inscribed temples appear to have documented their foundation by featuring a relief of the pharaoh and Seshat engaging in the act of "Stretching the Cord" or laying out the measurements for the new divine-dwelling. This was one of the most defining moments in the creation of any sanctuary, for the establishment of a temple resounded to the ruler's everlasting memory. Seshat was said to record these memories on a mythical Persea Tree. It was also her pen that made certain Pharaoh's relatively minor deeds resounded beyond his own lifetime and into the annals of Eternity.

Seshat was given special dominion in various areas where larger temples possessed libraries of sacred texts. It is for this reason that one of Seshat's titles was "Mistress of the House of Books." In these temple chambers, Seshat was said to dwell as patroness. Her cult images were possibly contained in small shrines or niches in these chambers, but her actual worship seems to have been primarily associated with the god Thoth, at Hermopolis. Cult personnel are indeed attested for Seshat, but it is not entirely clear if these priests were lodged in temples dedicated specifically to Seshat, or whether they were overseers in the sacred libraries of any given temple. Indeed, this goddess may not have possessed a *need* for a temple or cult of her own, owing to her intrinsic and honorary presence in every sanctuary from the moment sacred ground was "broken."

REMNANTS OF SESHAT: From the Delta to the remote regions of Nubia, you'll find imagery of Seshat in many significant temple ruins. At Abydos, however, there exists an especially striking testament to the official importance of this goddess. In the Temple of Seti I there is recorded an address from Seshat to the glorious pharaoh; this text is inscribed on a staircase leading from the temple to the hallowed annex known as the *Osireion.* Here, the goddess speaks of the "life" of the temple from the moment of its foundation to its consecration. She celebrates the various gods that dwell within, and the immortal pharaoh who acts as their High Priest. According to a decree of Ra-Atum, Seshat records this amazing work "for all posterity."

Tefnut

Chief Role: Goddess of Vengeance and Moisture
Chief Title: “The Distant One,” “Eye of Her Father Ra”
Cult Centers: Heliopolis, Leontopolis

Tefnut is an evasive goddess in many respects. She seems to have served so many different functions that it is sometimes difficult to tell what, exactly, she best personifies. It must be admitted that her mythical origins are intriguing; she and her brother-spouse, Shu, were either created by an act of masturbation on the part of their father, Atum, or were simply spit from his mouth. Their names are likely theological examples of onomatopoeia—the very sounds Atum made when he spit them out.

Not long after their mythical appearance in the cosmic realm, Tefnut and her spouse engendered Geb (Earth) and Nut (the Firmament) and took respective positions as personifications of the morning dew and the invisible atmosphere. Neither of these roles may seem very impressive, at first, but keep in mind that they likely had greater implications for the ancient theologian. Though the entire Heliopolitan clan should have settled into a happy cosmological existence, trouble began to brew. Geb not only lusted after his sister, Nut, but raped his mother, Tefnut, and stole the throne of his father, Shu! This tragedy was only the beginning. Tefnut, it appears, was one of the first of those very many goddesses said to embody the fiery Eye of Ra. One day, she was sent on the usual "rage across Egypt," much like Hathor, Sekhmet and other personalities. Tefnut's particular jaunt brought her all the way to distant Nubia.

Her prolonged absence sent the House of Ra into a state of frenzy. The great god decided to send Shu and Thoth to Nubia in an attempt to retrieve his daughter. To make certain that they could approach Tefnut without being too conspicuous, Ra recommended that the gods transform themselves into baboons. Presumably, in those days, two baboons sneaking up on you from behind was no cause for alarm.

When the simian posse reached Nubia, they discovered that Tefnut had been in the throes of a typical goddess-tantrum. Turning herself into a lioness (her sacred animal), she had satisfied her bloodlust by devouring the native populace and all the local wildlife. Thoth was finally able to use baboon magic and spellbinding stories to "lull" Tefnut into surrender and lure her back to Heliopolis. According to one version of the myth, a quick dunking in the Nile near the island of Bigeh served to cool her proverbial jets.

This tale of Tefnut's sojourn was, of course, a variant of other developed and widespread legends of Hathor-Sekhmet's rage. The importance of the story concerned the Nile flood and the relation of the fiery solar disc to this annual phenomenon; the "Eye" (as Tefnut) blazed a vicious trail all the way into Nubia, destroying crops with relentless ferocity. Upon return, it was a kinder, gentler sun. To reflect this pacification, the ancient Egyptians celebrated Tefnut's trip back home, complete with various mythical stops along the way. In the end, the calm Eye of Ra had returned and all was well with the world. This myth was also important to the cults of the deities Onuris and Menhyt—two leonine divinities of the delta who likely represented the "real" archaic identities of Shu and Tefnut before being processed and renamed by the neighboring Heliopolitan think-tank.

Some textual and inscriptional evidence exists to indicate that Tefnut demonstrated other solar qualities; in one portrayal she moves from Ra's Eye to his brow and becomes part of the *uraeus*. Her reputation as a leonine, volatile goddess would have facilitated this concept. While Tefnut's role as goddess of "condensation" does seem a bit miniscule or ridiculous, it should be remembered that the Egyptians didn't get a great deal of rain. Every bit of morning dew or moisture was appreciated. Indeed, an obscure passage from the Pyramid Texts claims that Tefnut generated a flow of water from her genitals, intended to cool the feet of the Pharaoh. On her way back from Nubia, the pacified Tefnut was also less apt to burn away every trace of valuable moisture retained by the land for the benefit of a good crop. In other texts, Tefnut is sometimes said to act as a protectress of the dead, quenching their thirst with her "moistening" talents or sometimes bestowing the breath of life upon them, but this funerary role was certainly not unique to her personality.

It seems likely that Tefnut originated as a local goddess with a specific cult of her own before joining the Heliopolitan Ennead. While one might posit a Nubian origin for the goddess, it is far more likely that she came Sebennytos or Leontopolis, a town very near Heliopolis. Fitting for a place that the Greeks dubbed "City of the Lion," a number of leonine gods were venerated there, especially the great deity Aker. Shu, in his own primitive form as a leonine god, possessed a joint sanctuary with Tefnut at Leontopolis and the two were already likely associated when the Heliopolitan theologians appropriated them.

As mentioned, it is very likely that Tefnut was a personality derived from the goddess Menhyt, who also dwelled near Heliopolis and acted as the raging Eye of Ra. Her consort, Onuris, was a most august and ancient god with a name meaning "He Who Brings Back the Distant [Goddess]." According to one strain of the Onuris legend, Ra's Eye was actually sent out to recover Shu and Tefnut when they accidentally tumbled into the Great Abyss. Upon return, the "Menhyt Eye" was infuriated to discover that another "Eye" had taken her place—hence her own pouty trip to Nubia.

Heliopolis would remain Tefnut's primary cult center and her specific inclusion as a chief goddess of the district is indicated by ancient inscriptions that name Ra, Shu and Tefnut as three deities who always "dwelled" in Anu, the ancient name of Heliopolis. It is said that the magnificent solar temple at Heliopolis was home to two sacred lions that were considered to be the living incarnations of Atum-Ra's firstborn children. A special sanctuary for Shu and Tefnut *is* attested in history of the city.

REMNANTS OF TEFNUT: Outside the lost monuments of Heliopolis and Leontopolis, one of the only extant temples dedicated to Tefnut is the sanctuary at Esna, which was apparently a stopping point on her mythical journey from

Nubia, back home to Ra. Of course, Tefnut was closely identified with Menhyt in this temple and the edifice was the home of many other deities as well. In Ptolemaic times, however, Tefnut was the object of popular auxiliary cults at Edfu, Abydos, Dendera, Kom Ombo, and especially around the First Cataract region. At Bigeh Island, she was equated and venerated as a form of Hathor. On Philae, the island of her granddaughter Isis, the intrepid wanderer will note that Tefnut was quite prominently paired with a Shu-like Nubian deity called "Arensnuphis." The relationship with Arensnuphis assured for Tefnut a fine place in temple reliefs at Kalabsha, El-Dakkah, and several other sites south of the First Cataract. Of these structures, the temple of Kalabsha is certainly worth a visit with a well-versed guide.

Wadjet

Chief Role: Uraeus Goddess and Patroness of Lower Egypt
Chief Title: "The Green One"
Cult Centers: Buto, Avaris

Wadjet was arguably the ancient Egyptian cobra-goddess *par excellence,* a divinity that rose from obscurity in the marshes near the Mediterranean to a place of lasting national honor. Like her counterpart, the vulture-goddess Nekhbet in the south, Wadjet came to literally personify the Royal Crown of her geographical sphere. She was selected for this role due to the strength and antiquity of her cult in the Delta city of Pr-Wadjet. This is the place where the legendary "Bee Kings" supposedly decided to rule during the Archaic Period of Egyptian history. That the name of the goddess actually seems to mean "The Green One" indicates the status of her city as a chief port on the greenish waters of the Mediterranean and/or its proximity to the lush green papyrus swamps of the Delta as a whole.

It might be said that Wadjet first achieved fame as the chief "fashion accessory" of Ra himself. The sun god knew that one certain way to thwart his enemies was to wear a living cobra upon his head and Wadjet was the right goddess for the task. Fixed upon the brow of Ra, Wadjet's venom was potent when she lashed out at foes. This power allowed the cult of Wadjet to assume a number of solar qualities and motifs. Therefore, as the sun's rays burned the faces of working Egyptians, so did Wadjet's fire and poison burn up the eyes, faces, and opponents of Pharaoh. For this reason, the rulers of Lower Egypt appear to have adapted the *uraeus* to their crowns as a sign that they—like Ra—were under the protection of this highly dangerous goddess.

Fearsome Patroness of the Pharaoh

Wadjet's neighboring Delta goddess, Neith, was also portrayed wearing the Red Crown of Lower Egypt, but it must have been a better fit on the cobra-goddess, for Wadjet gained at least an honorary identification with the Crown and tutelary status as Nekhbet's northern alter ego. Wadjet's city and Neith's cult center at

Sais were important political and economic centers of the "Crossed Bows" Nome and the two goddesses were probably considered to be different dimensions of the same personality. Though their character-traits could be quite different, the two would be intimately linked, in certain respects, well into the New Kingdom and beyond (see the article about Neith). Wadjet was also honored with an important temple at Avaris during the Ramesside period, further evidence of her dominion in key parts of the Nile Delta.

Even after the port city of Pr-Wadjet silted-up and lost its prime economic status, the region retained a religious significance as home to symbolic rites connected with the pharaoh's ascension to the throne. Indeed, Wadjet's most important moment came during the installation of a new king. She was ever depicted in iconography and reliefs placing the proper geographical crown upon the ruler's head, with Nekhbet doing the same on the opposite side. Though often depicted strictly in serpentine form, temple artists wisely gave Wadjet an anthropomorphic body to complete this crucial function. If the contemporary visitor is careful to look, he or she will see Wadjet on every crown worn in the iconography of gods and royals alike.

After the New Kingdom, Wadjet was one of many goddesses who entered the Osirian legend as a rather solicitous immortal who ventured near the infant, Horus, in the Delta marshlands offering protection from the evil

Set. In this story, Wadjet was said to have transformed her hair into bulrushes and reeds, covering the babe that he might escape detection. To secure her own escape from Set, Wadjet was also said to have had the power to transform herself into a shrew—an animal that may have been a sacred fetish in her cult from early times. One may rightfully speculate that this rodent was also a favorite snack and offering to the cobras likely (and carefully) kept in the temple precinct of Wadjet. Wadjet's involvement in the Osirian myth may also reflect an ancient reality concerning the actual layout of her city. Pr-Wadjet was actually a dual community, with one district (Dep) being dedicated to the cult of a certain manifestation of Horus, while the other (Pe) was the sole domain of Wadjet the Cobra.

Wadjet of the Oracle

In Ptolemaic times, the Greeks took a liking to Wadjet, though they changed her name to the more pronounceable "Uto." From the pylon of her renowned temple, the vast Mediterranean could be seen in the distance. In this temple, Wadjet (or more appropriately, her priests) demonstrated prophetic talents; in latter times the sanctuary of Wadjet became the site of a renowned oracle that persisted well into the era of Roman occupation. Judging from the earlier account of Herodotus, Wadjet's oracle was every bit as reputable in its day as was the oracle belonging to Amun at Siwah Oasis.

Indeed, the famed Greek historian visited Wadjet's sanctuary and was notably impressed by its *naos,* which was carved from one immense block of Aswan granite. Herodotus was also enamored of the mysterious Island of Khemmis, situated in a "lake" not far from the Wadjet enclosure. The locals swore to Herodotus that the sacred island actually "floated" upon the surface of the lake and was holy because Wadjet had once hidden the child Horus there as a favor to the persecuted Isis.

REMNANTS OF WADJET: There isn't much to see. It's a bit sad, given the great importance of this goddess. However, if you were an ancient traveler heading northwest away from Sais and toward the Mediterranean, you would have swiftly found yourself in Wadjet territory. Within the walls of her city, the citizens of Buto would have proudly informed you of their goddess and her unique prerogatives. Certainly, you would have seen glimpses of her splendid temple from the exterior of the enclosure walls. As it is today, the the modern town of Tell Fara'un is lacking in both cobras and notable remains of the temple of Wadjet. However, there *are* remains of a Wadjet shrine near Imet. Oddly enough, Wadjet was also one of the many deities worshipped in the distant temple of Mandulis at Kalabsha. There, she was associated with the Nubian sun-god as consort. Despite their shared solar qualities, one wonders how the mighty northern goddess made her way so deeply into southern territory at such a late stage of her career.

~Appendices~

A Gathering of "Honorable Mentions"

AMMUT "She Who Devours the Dead" was *not* the most beloved goddess of the ancient Egyptians, but she was quite well known in folklore and, probably, more than one nightmare. As a flesh-eating denizen of Duat, the underworld, Ammut waited for the results of the Weighing of the Heart ritual In the *Book of the Dead* she appears as a hideous amalgamation of crocodile, lioness, and hippopotamus forms. It was her job to devour the heart of any deceased soul that failed to meet the demands of eternal justice.

BAT This deity was a very ancient bovine goddess worshiped in her own city, which was called "Hwt" (Diospolis Parva to the Greeks). Bat's human face, or that of possible cultic-cousin, Hathor—adorned with cow's ears—appeared quite early in full-frontal fashion on the Palette of Narmer. Bat's fetish, the sistrum, was honored at Hwt in a temple called the Mansion of the Sistrum and was at some point stylized as a ritual rattle and associated with several other Egyptian goddesses. It is thought that, by the onset of the Middle Kingdom, Bat was absorbed by the personality of Hathor in the city and nome of Hwt. In Greco-Roman times, Nephthys appears with Hathor (or *as* Hathor) in the role as chief goddess of the Mansion of the Sistrum.

HAT-MEHIT The fish-faced Hat-Mehit was the original and most important deity of the great Delta city of Mendes. When the ram-headed god Banebdjet was made chieftain of Mendes, Hat-Mehit was subordinated as his consort. In Ptolemaic times, Hat-Mehit was identified with Isis and considered to be a mother of one form of Horus. She thus received a special cult at the famed Isis temple at Behbeit. Both Mendes and Behbeit were apparently destroyed in a massive earthquake, perhaps in the early days of the Roman Occupation.

HESAT Hesat was an ancient cow-goddess of a city the Greeks later called Aphroditopolis. It was believed that she provided milk for Pharaoh's nourishment when he was in calf-form. Like so many other bovine deities, Hesat was associated with cosmic creation and eventually absorbed by the ever-popular Hathor.

MEHEURET This cow-goddess was nicknamed "The Great Flood," for it was said that she was the immense waterway upon which Atum-Ra traversed the Firmament. Neith and Hathor absorbed this goddess in later Dynasties.

MENHYT A powerful and ferocious goddess, Menhyt was normally depicted in the form of a lioness. In her rebellious role as the Eye of Ra she appears as a form of (or possible derivation of) Tefnut. She was associated with the god

Onuris and worshiped at Sebennytos, though she appears at Sais with Neith and at Esna with Khnum in late times. The importance of her affiliate-goddess, Mehyt, in the temple of Edfu cannot be underemphasized.

PAKHET A leonine goddess who was likely a form of Sekhmet, Pakhet was especially honored in the days of Hatshepsut at an isolated, cave-like temple near modern Beni Hassan. Inscriptions at this beguiling shrine describe Pakhet as "She Who Scratches" and "She Whose Pathways are Storm-Beaten."

RAYET This goddess appears at Heliopolis as the female consort of Ra himself. Though she doesn't seem to have caused much of a stir elsewhere, Raet and a related goddess called Nebethetepet possessed their own sanctuaries and priests. The citizens of Heliopolis believed that Raet was highly skilled in magic.

RONPET In Greco-Roman times, this otherwise obscure goddess was popular among Egyptian women as a bestower of youth and vitality. Her emblem was the notched palm-branch.

SOTHIS This goddess was one of the most ancient in Egypt, appearing as the personification of the "Dogstar" and thus as a harbinger of the inundation. In character she most resembles the Cataract goddess Satis, but her identity was almost completely absorbed by Isis in later periods.

TAWERET Depicted in the form of a great female hippopotamus, Taweret was one of Egypt's most popular household divinities, particularly in her capacity as a protectress of childbirth. Though she could have an ominous nature at times, and was paired with Set as concubine, Taweret was more often associated with joyful, mischievous gods like Bes. In her form as the goddess Opet, she possessed a popular little temple at Thebes where Osirian rites were performed. She was also honored with a temple in the Fayyum region during the Ramesside period.

TAYET This goddess was the patroness of weavers and spinners, worshipped alongside her consort Min in the city of Akhmim, the center of ancient Egyptian linen production. At Busiris and elsewhere, she takes on a dualistic form as "Shentayet" and appears to be primarily identified with Isis (and sometimes Nephthys) as the maker of the Osirian funerary garments—a role also ascribed to Neith in certain legends.

UNNUT Despite having the head of a rabbit, Unnut was thought to be quite fierce and brandished two daggers in various ancient inscriptions to prove it. A rather archaic but apparently important deity of the Hermopolite Nome, little is known of her. Unnut's cult and temple were seemingly usurped by Thoth in early Dynastic times.

A Survey of Some Primary Goddess Cult-Centers

This survey does not purport to cover every cult center of every Egyptian goddess, but will hopefully give the intrepid wanderer a summary of some of the main worship-sites mentioned in the prior articles of this book. Always check with *official* government/tourist agencies and reputable travel companies before planning a trip to Egypt and certainly before visiting any Egyptian city or site.

Alexandria
Chief Goddess: Isis

The glorious city built at the behest of Alexander the Great and graced by charismatic Cleopatra VII was certainly one of the most magnificent of the ancient world. It's a shame that relatively little is left to remind us of former splendor. The Greco-Egyptian hybrid deity, Serapis, was the master of the city, his cult tailored for the metropolis and introduced by Ptolemy I Soter. A stunning, gold-encrusted sanctuary was built for the avuncular god and this temple remained the greatest in the region until its destruction by Christians in 391 CE.

Before the Christian onslaught, however, Alexandria boasted a diverse religious landscape. Isis was by far the supreme goddess of the district; several temples were built in her honor and statues of the goddess were erected everywhere. Other deities were represented by cults as well—Anubis, Hathor, Poseidon, Hephaestus and Aphrodite among them. The good news is that antiquities are constantly being discovered through excavation of present sites and exploration of the extensive harbor that now covers what were once the ancient city's streets and monuments. In 1996, for example, archaeologists discovered what they believe to have been part of Cleopatra's palace in twenty feet of bay-water. In 2002, the remains of the ancient city and temple of Herakleion were discovered twelve miles out to sea!

Antaeopolis (Qaw al-Kebir)
Chief Goddess: Nephthys

This town once boasted an exceedingly lovely Ptolemaic temple dedicated to an exceedingly violent deity named Anti or Antiwey, whom the Greeks identified with their legendary wrestling giant, Antaios. For the Egyptians, this god represented the explosive, warrior-like fusion of Horus and Set in one package. The goddess originally associated with this city may have been fiery Mehyt but, in the Late Period, cult personnel for Nephthys are attested here. Isis was also worshipped in the district. Though an ancient necropolis still boasts archaeologically significant tombs from early dynasties and the Roman period, the once large and stately temple was washed away by Nile waters in the 19th century. It's a shame—the site would have been a major attraction, had even the ruins somehow been preserved. However, two enigmatic paintings of Antaios and Nephthys can still be seen in a nearby stone quarry to this day, guarding their domain.

Aphroditopolis
Chief Goddess: Hathor, Hesat

This city was known as Pr-Hathor in very ancient times, even though another bovine goddess—Hesat—was the original deity of the region. A splendid temple (perhaps dating from Dynasty II) occupied the center of the town and, when the Greeks arrived, it was here that they most prominently identified Hathor with Aphrodite, their own goddess of beauty. The crocodilian god Sobek was venerated in the vicinity, though none of his ruins remain.

Aswan
Chief Goddess: Satis, Anukis, Isis

Khnum, the ram-headed Lord of Elephantine Island was the principal god of exotic Aswan, but his consorts, Satis and Anukis, were probably established in the area before he came along. From an early time, Aswan was a significant religious and commercial center, owing to its status as a frontier town and military outpost. In Ptolemaic times, when Isis-worship dominated the First Cataract region, Khnum and his goddesses gave way to the

Osirian family, with whom they were conveniently identified.

Even though Isis was supreme in the end, her little Ptolemaic temple in Aswan is something of an architectural dud. In this temple she is equated with Satis while her sister, Nephthys, is equated with Anukis. Much nicer are the Hathor and Mandulis temples transplanted from Nubian sites after the building of the Aswan High Dam. New excavations are underway, and interesting ruins are still being unearthed.

Busiris
Chief Goddess: Isis-Shentayet, Nephthys-Shentayet

Many scholars believe that Busiris was the first cult-center of the great Osiris and that it fell from primacy only after national attention shifted to Abydos. Throughout its history, however, Busiris radiated holiness as the reputed burial place of the "djed" pillar—a relic thought to symbolize the occipital backbone of the murdered Osiris, but which was more likely a fetish first associated with Ptah and Sokar, signifying the concept of eternal stability.

A great festival was held annually at Busiris, re-enacting the troubles of Osiris and his family. The "Passion Play" must have been convincing, for Herodotus tells us that anguished pilgrims flagellated themselves in their grief. Isis and Nephthys were the chief goddesses of Busiris, especially in their forms as "weaving goddesses." Also honored here were Horus and Sokar. No significant temple remnants exist.

Buto
Chief Goddess: Wadjet

Called "Pr-Wadjet" in ancient times, this was the abode of Egypt's greatest cobra-goddess. Menhyt was a goddess venerated in this district as well. Half of the city belonged officially to Wadjet while the other half was dedicated to a form of Horus. Today, nothing remains of the legendary temple lauded by Herodotus except a few crumbling walls and walkways.

Dakleh Oasis
Chief Goddess: Tapsais, Mut, Nephthys, Isis, etc.

Many groupings of gods were adored in the isolated but exotic region that comprised Dakhleh Oasis and its neighboring communities. The state cults of Amun-Re and Mut were very important, but so were the local cults of Neith, Tapsais, and the Osirian family of gods. Set and Nephthys were worshipped as "Lords" of the oasis as well, for their domain was the outer edge of the desert world.

Damanhur
Chief Goddess: Neith

This city was originally sacred to Horus, but a few artifacts from Dynasty XXX, including a naos of Neith, are now on display in the Cairo Museum. During the Greco-Roman age this town shared the name “Hermopolis Parva” with the famed capital of Nome XV of Lower Egypt. Thus, it is likely that the god Thoth shared a place of honor here along with Horus and Neith.

Deir el-Bahri
Chief Goddess: Hathor-Mertseger

This place is the site of a temple dedicated to the mortuary cult of the legendary Queen Hatshepsut, and is one of the most stunning extant examples of ancient architectural design in the world. Here, Hatshepsut honored the gods Hathor-Mertseger and Anubis with special annexed chapels.

Deir Al-Madinah
Chief Goddess: Mertseger, Hathor, Maat

This “lost city” was originally founded as a community for necropolis workers. The sanctuary here (built mostly by Ptolemy IV long after the decline of the town) is tiny but interesting, as it is dedicated to an unusual group of deities: Hathor, Maat, and Imhotep among them. Of equal interest to archaeologists are the scattered workers’ tombs boasting scenes of ancient funerary rites and attendant deities. Other gods sacred in the vicinity were Osiris, Anubis, Renenutet, and Thoth. The queen of them all, however, was Mertseger—

serpentine protectress and personification of the eerie "Peak of the West."

Dendara
Chief Goddess: Hathor

Dendara was the primary cult town of Hathor from the earliest Dynastic periods. The well-preserved Ptolemaic temple of the goddess standing here now was the last of perhaps many temples erected to Hathor on this holy spot. Raised between 125 BCE and 60 CE, the huge (though unfinished) edifice was also dedicated to Horus of Edfu and their offspring, Ihy and Harsomtus.

Diospolis Parva (Hiw)
Chief Goddess: Nephthys

Simply called "Hwt" or "Mansion of the Sistrum" in ancient times, this city seems to have known a succession of patron goddesses and diverse cults, depending upon the era. The bovine goddess Bat was first established here, perhaps from the time of King Narmer. During the Middle Kingdom she was absorbed by Hathor. Later, when the town housed the Osirian family and a sanctuary of the Sacred Phoenix, *Hwt* was said to be the birthplace of Nephthys, who rendered special protective duties to both Osiris and the Bennu Bird in her form of Kherseket. It was only when Nephthys assimilated the personality traits of Hathor in Greco-Roman times, however, that Diospolis

Parva and its nome became her fiefdom. She was associated here with the youthful god Neferhotep.

Edfu
Chief Goddess: Hathor

The Temple of Horus (begun by the Ptolemies in 237 BCE) is second only to the temple of Karnak in extant grandeur and is much more well-preserved. The holiness of the site stems from a belief that Horus defeated Set in a great battle nearby. Resplendent and lonesome, the temple remains one of Egypt's greatest attractions. The chief goddess at Edfu was Hathor, spouse of Horus, but many other goddesses associated with the Osirian family and the solar cult were worshipped here as well. Mehyt was perhaps foremost of these adjunct deities.

Elephantine Island
Chief Goddess: Satis, Anukis

Elephantine Island was the chief center for the worship of the inundation deities; its temples were the main attraction near the First Cataract until Isis came to prominence at nearby Philae. Before this, priests of Khnum, Satis, and Anukis were powerful landowners in charge of interpreting the "nilometer," a device that monitored the level of the annual flood. Satis was probably the original deity of the isle (perhaps along with Hapy) and her temple was recently rebuilt by a team of diligent German archaeologists. It dates from the time of Hatshepsut. The temples to Khnum and Anukis are in a much greater state of ruin.

Esna
Chief Goddess: Neith, Menhyt, Nebtu'u

Esna was the seat of the Upper Egyptian cult of Khnum, the ram-headed god of the inundation. It was also the site of a unique creationist cosmology involving Khnum and the very ancient Delta goddess Neith. The large but partially excavated temple was finished under Roman rule and its walls proclaim the local prominence of several goddesses, especially Nebtu'u and the Tefnut-derivative, Menhyt.

Fayyum
Chief Goddess: Isis-Renenutet

The Fayyum Oasis belonged primarily to the crocodilian god, Sobek, whose cult held great fascination for Ptolemaic and Roman rulers, as well as *ancient* tourists. The Greco-Romans refurbished Sobek's shrines and introduced their own versions of the already established deity. Goddesses were important in the Fayyum as well; Neith was associated with Sobek early on and later a similar relationship was forged with the goddess Isis-Renenutet. A few scant ruins exist today, but are not necessarily worth a visit.

Heliopolis
Chief Goddess: Isis, Tefnut, Nut, Hathor, Raet, Nebethetepet

As one of ancient Egypt's primary theological centers, the Heliopolitan priests maintained their reputation for wisdom long after their city had been overshadowed by Thebes. Ra-Atum-Kephri ruled supreme in a pyramid-style solar temple, but the goddesses of his famous Ennead were ever at his side: Tefnut, Nut, Isis, Nephthys. Hathor was also a chieftain goddess on her own at Heliopolis. Ra's consort-goddesses Raet and Nebethetepet also enjoyed cults in the legendary City of the Sun. Though it was once a place of astonishing religious splendor, nothing much remains today except a solitary obelisk.

Imaou (Kom al-Hisn)
Chief Goddess: Hathor-Sekhmet

This community was the capital of Nome III of Lower Egypt during the New Kingdom and eventually became a necropolis under the Hyksos Kings. Ramses II, Amenemhet II, and Sheshonk II did some building here and a number of archaeological finds have emerged from the rubble. These are now on display at the Cairo Museum. The local goddess cult must have packed a punch, as it was dedicated to the most intimidating goddess-fusion ever: Hathor-Sekhmet.

Iseum (Behbeit el-Hagar)
Chief Goddess: Isis

The name of the ancient cult town of Hebitet meant "Domain of the Festive [Goddess]" and was a place devoted to the rites and offerings which Isis "set down" to enact the resurrection of Osiris. She was essentially her husband's mistress of ceremonies. The Nectanebo Pharaohs and then the Ptolemies built a truly splendid sanctuary in which Isis could properly look after her husband, with the help of Horus, Anubis, and the usual Osirian suspects. Built almost entirely from Aswan granite and boasting some of the most extraordinary reliefs of the period, the entire temple came crashing down (likely in an earthquake) before 80 CE. Today, the place is a haunting heap of blocks and scattered columns. Archaeologists hope to someday make full excavation of the shrine.

Kom Ombo
Chief Goddess: Hathor, Tasenetnofret

The riverbanks of this ancient city were a favored gathering place for the Nile crocodile, so it was only natural that a deity like Sobek reigned as the chief god. The graceful temple (also dedicated, via "dual axis," to the falcon-headed Haroeris) still attracts tourists by the boatload. At the setting of the sun the ruins take on a stunning, almost unsettling aura. The temple "crocodile pool" is a must-see. Hathor enjoyed a cult at Kom Ombo, along with an obscure local goddess who seemed to have been a derivative of Hathor or Tefnut and whose epithet was simply, "The Beautiful Sister."

Komir
Chief Goddess: Nephthys and Anukis

This site was primarily excavated in 1978 but its temple had long been known due to inscriptions in the temple of Khnum at Esna twelve kilometers to the north. The ancients knew this as a cult center of the goddess Anukis, whose sacred animal, the gazelle, inhabited the desert region and was buried in a special gazelle-necropolis. Probably beginning in the Late Period, as Esna enjoyed typical Osirian significance, the cult of Nephthys was introduced and she became co-owner of the temple at Komir. The present ruined temple of Nephthys and Anukis preserves eloquent hymns to both goddesses and dates from the reign of Emperor Antoninus Pius.

Koptos (Qift)
Chief Goddess: Isis

This ancient mining community was a chief city of the ithyphallic god Min, who supposedly protected routes to the distant quarries. A temple of Min was likely in existence here as early as Dynasty IV, endowed by subsequent pharaohs as the commercial importance of Koptos grew with the expansion of aforementioned routes. Isis was enthusiastically worshipped here as the co-equal and consort of Min in a temple they shared, dating from at least the New Kingdom. During annual celebrations, women of Koptos were, at one point, said to walk barefoot through scorpion-filled pits as proof of their faith in the protection of Isis.

Mendes (Tell al-Ruba)
Chief Goddess: Hat-Mehit, Isis

This Delta locale was originally the estate of a fish-headed goddess called Hat-Mehit, but at an early date the ram-headed god Banebdjet usurped her temple and relegated her to more of a wifely status. Together, however, they ruled sacred Mendes until the Osirian camp absorbed their prerogatives and identified themselves with the resident gods in the Late Period.

Memphis
Chief Goddess: Sekhmet, Neith, Hathor, Isis, Bastet, etc.

The splendor of this first (and most enduring) imperial city in history was once legendary. As a religious capital, Memphis boasted its own creationist theology to rival that of Heliopolis, and was likely built on a scale to rival Thebes. Ptah was chief god, along with his consort Sekhmet. Neith, Isis, and Hathor also owned temple property at various periods in Memphite history. It is one of archaeology's greatest losses that only scant ruins of this once-glorious religious center are to be found at the site today.

Naukratis
Chief Goddess: Neith

There is a stele on display at the Cairo Museum in which the temple of Neith at Sais is guaranteed (by decree of Pharaoh) a ten percent tariff on all goods imported through this famed ancient port-city. The fact that an exact duplicate of that stele was discovered in 2002, twelve miles out to sea in the submerged ruins of ancient Heraklieon, indicates that the king meant business and Neith was *not* to be short-changed in the Delta region. Ever.

Nekheb
Chief Goddess: Nekhbet

This archaic city was important because of its proximity to the Horus-ruled "capital" at nearby Nekhen. Later on, Nekheb actually became the more prosperous of the two locales. The vulture goddess Nekhbet was supreme here, honored with a massive temple dating at least from the time of Amenhotep II and Ramses II. Sobek shared space with Nekhbet in her city and Thoth was honored with a sanctuary or two. In Ptolemaic times, Nekhbet was assimilated to Hathor and several chapels were erected in honor of this fusion.

Oxyrhynchus
Chief Goddess: Isis, Taweret

Once the capital of the nineteenth nome of Upper Egypt, this city—later famed for its troves of papyrus documents—was home to many gods. Set was worshipped here, along with his concubine goddess, Taweret. In Greco-Roman times, however, Osiris, Isis, and a host of Greek deities were honored with temples.

Panopolis (Akhmim)
Chief Goddess: Repyet, Isis-Tayet

Once the capital of Nome IX of Upper Egypt, Panopolis was dedicated to Min, whom the Greeks confused with their own god, Pan. The town was also sacred to Repyet-Tayet, Min's wife. Scant remains of the temples can still be seen, most dating from Dynasty XVIII and the Ptolemaic period. As a commercial center of linen production, Panopolis was also sacred to Isis-Tayet, goddess of the loom.

Philae
Chief Goddess: Isis

Famed Philae was the last bastion of ancient Egyptian religion. Not until 535 CE did the emperor Justinian give orders to close the Temple of Isis. Ironically, this island came into religious prominence only at a late period in ancient Egyptian history. An Osiris cult was maintained on the large nearby island of Bigeh and, beginning with Pharaoh Ahmasis, construction work on the little isle of Philae began so Isis could presumably "tend" to her husband across the water. The general popularity of Isis, however, swiftly overshadowed any cultic veneration of her husband and associated deities. All the rest became mere props for *her* adoration. By the time of Christ, the temple of Isis at Philae was one of the most powerful temples—politically and economically—in all of Egypt.

The temple still stands and, though far from the largest or most exquisitely decorated in Egypt, it is probably the most bewitching. Ostensibly established by Nectanebo II, the central sanctuary was enlarged over the centuries by subsequent Ptolemaic and Roman rulers. These men added a great cluster of chapels, kiosks, colonnades and shrines, mostly dedicated to obscure Nubian gods. Within the main temple, the walls are covered with reliefs of the pharaohs offering to the chief resident gods: Isis, Osiris, Hathor, Horus, and Nephthys. Like the Abu Simbel temple-site in southern Nubia, Philae's temples were dismantled and rescued in the early 1980s from annual flooding by waters raised due to construction of the Aswan dam. Everything was transported intact to the nearby high-and-dry isle of Agilkia.

Sais
Chief Goddess: Neith

Sais was one of Egypt's oldest and most prestigious cities and Neith's was a very powerful national cult, but one would never guess it from what is left. During Dynasty XXVI, Sais was the capital of all Egypt. Herodotus himself described the splendor of Neith's temple when he visited in the fifth century BCE. The Osirian cult was once supreme here, as well; by the Late Period, Isis had become identified with Neith at Sais.

Sebennytos
Chief Goddess: Menhyt

Nectanebo II built the great, now-destroyed temple at Sebennytos and dedicated it to the popular warrior god, Onuris. His wife, the ferocious goddess Menhyt, received cultic worship in the temple as well. As a raging lioness, she was one of the most deserving divinities honored with the ubiquitous epithet, "Eye of Ra."

Sehil Island
Chief Goddess: Anukis

This island near the First Cataract was specifically sacred to the consorts of Khnum, but Anukis was honored here before any of the others. Today, Sehil Island is best known for its abundance of ancient graffiti and very fragmentary remains of an Anukis shrine.

Speos Artemidos (Beni Hasan)
Chief Goddess: Pakhet

Queen Hatshepsut established a charming rock-hewn temple for the feral leonine goddess, Pakhet, in this desert place. When the Greeks arrived they equated Pakhet with their huntress deity, Artemis. Today, the Middle Kingdom rock-cut tombs are the main attraction at Beni Hasan, mainly because the little temple itself is well off the beaten path.

Sepermeru
Chief Goddess: Nephthys

This town, situated between Oxyrhynchus to the south and Herakleopolis to the north, was the capital of Nome XIX of Upper Egypt before administration later shifted to Oxyrhynchus. The place was sacred to Set, but Ramesess II built a temple for Nephthys here, as well. Both deities were apparently guardians of Ra-Harakhte, who likewise possessed an outlying shrine at Sepermeru.

Taposiris Magna (Abu Sir)
Chief Goddess: Isis

This Delta city was sacred to the whole Osirian family, like so many other towns. The temple of Osiris (built by Ptolemy II) is extant, though there's nothing much to see except a crumbling pylon and the ruined courtyard. Naturally, the Osirian *milieu* of goddesses was honored here, led by Isis.

Thebes (Karnak-Luxor)
Chief Goddess: Mut-Sekhmet-Hathor-Bastet, Opet, Amaunet, Maat

The greatest religious-imperial capital in ancient history must be *seen* to be believed. The war god, Montu, was the primary deity here until the Dynasty XI (or XII) ascendancy of Amun. The goddess Mut was a likely presence here or in the Theban suburbs at the outset, too, possibly along with the minor lunar-god, Khons. Once Amun became surpreme at Thebes, the religious landscape of Egypt would never be the same.

Many of the greatest pharaohs of Egypt tried to leave their mark on this most magnificent of religious centers. As companion-goddess of Amun-Ra, Mut rated her own enormous precinct near a sacred lake called Asheru. Here, she was linked inseparably with Sekhmet, whose statues filled the courts and continue to haunt the ruins to this very day. Hathor was long-worshipped here and in the various funerary cult-temples, as was the motherly goddess, Opet, and Amun's original "wife," Amaunet.

Little Map of the Ancient Goddess Cult-Centers

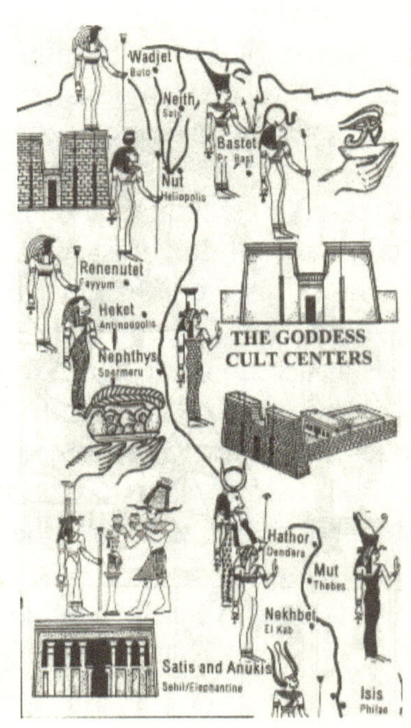

Some Primary Festivals of the Ancient Egyptian Calendar

The Ancient Egyptian Calendar was divided into three chief seasons with various months. Each locality had festivals and feasts peculiar to its deities and traditions. Following are only some of the noted feasts celebrated during the course of the Egyptian calendar year, many of them relating on both local and national levels to the deities described in this book. The historical dating of these feasts, due to the passage of antiquity, must always be considered approximate, at best.

Akhet (Season of the Flood)

First Month

1st Day—New Year's Day and the birthday of Ra-Horakhte

15th Day—Feast of offerings to Hapy and Amun for the Inundation

18th Day—Wag Feast of Osiris

19th Day—Feast of Wag and Thoth

20th Day—Feast of Drunkenness

22nd Day—Feast of the Great Procession of Osiris

Second Month

15th Day—Feast of Ipet in Luxor

19th Day—Feast of Ipet and Feast Days of Amun's Celebration

18th Day—Feast of Khnum and Anukis

27th Day—Feast of Montu at Thebes

28th Day—Feast of Satis and Anukis at Elephantine

Additional Feast Day: Feast of Ptah of Memphis, South of His Wall

Third Month

9th Day—Feast Days of Amun Beginning

30th Day—Feast of Anukis of Elephantine,

Additional Feast—Great Feast of the Beginning of Hathor's Journey

Fourth Month

1st Day—Feast of Hathor on Her Boat

18th Day—Beginning of the Feast of Khoiak and the Osirian Rites

22nd Day—Feast of Ploughing the Earth

26th Day—Feast of Sokar and His Bark

30th Day—Feast of the Raising of the Djed Totem

Peret, the Spring (Season of Growing)

First Month

1st Day—Feast of Nehebkau the Beginning of Eternity

20th Day—Feast of the Bark of Wadjet at Asheru

29th Day—Feast of the Bark of Bast at Asheru

29th Day—Feast of the Willow

30th Day—Feast of the Bark of Shesmet at Asheru

Additional Feasts:

Feast of Mut Mistress of Asheru
Feast of the Crowning of Horus of Edfu
Feast of the Return of the Distant Goddess

Second Month

1st Day—Feast of the Bark of Anubis

30th Day—Feast of "Amun Who Raises Heaven"

Additonal Feast—Feast of the Triumph of Horus of Edfu

Third Month

1st Day—Feast of Ptah of Thebes and Feast of the Return of "Amun Who Raises Heaven"

21st Day—Feast of Pharaoh Amenhotep I at Thebes

29th Day—Feast Days of Pharaoh Amenhotep I at the Necropolis of Deir al-Madinah

Fourth Month

4th Day—Feast of Bastet

5th Day—Feast of Bast Who Sails in Her Bark

25th Day—Feast of Harvest Offerings to Renenutet

27th Day—Feast of Granary Offerings to Renenutet

28th Day—Feast of the Heart of Nephthys at Edfu Rejoicing

Shomu (Season of Harvesting)

First Month

1st Day—Feast of Renenutet Who Gives Birth to Nepri

10th Day—Feast of the Adoration of Anubis

11th Day—Feast of Min in His Departure

Additional Feasts:
Feast of Khons
Feast of Hathor "Who Brings Forth"

Second Month

Feast of the Beautiful Valley at Thebes

Third Month

15th Day—Feast of the Offerings to Hapy and Amun of the Inundation

30th Day—Eve of the Feast of Beautiful Meeting of Horus and Hathor

Fourth Month

24th Day—Feast of Ptah at Memphis

30th Day—Feast of the Eve of the New Year

Feast of the New Year

Additional Feast—Feast of Ra-Horakhte

Epagomenal/Intercalary Days

Feast of Osiris
Feast of Haroeris
Feast of Set
Feast of Isis
Feast of Nephthys

The Western Portion of the Ancient Nile Delta

The Eastern Portion of the Ancient Nile Delta

Ancient Sites of Lower and Middle Egypt

Middle Egyptian Temple-Sites

Upper Egyptian Sites: Akhmim to Thebes

Upper Egypt from Esna to Kom Ombo

The Sacred First Cataract Region of Upper Egypt

This famed statue of the goddess Amaunet, consort of Amun-Ra, is found amid the ruins of Karnak Temple and dates from the reign of King Tutankhamun.

Located near the Sixth Pylon in the famed Record Hall of Thutmose III, the presence of Amaunet's beautiful statue indicates that she maintained her prestige as a goddess of Thebes even after the ascent of the great goddess Mut.

This photograph captures the prow of the Sacred Ritual Bark of Isis from her temple on the island of Philae.

Each major god and goddess owned a sacred boat used in various rituals and feasts connected with a particular temple. The barks could vary in size, depending upon the wealth of the temple estate, but all were considered to be the chief means of transporting the resident cult-image during Nile processions and "visits" to deities in other temples. The head of the god or goddess was normally depicted on the prow of the bark as a sign of ownership.

Hathor was worshipped throughout Egypt and in all periods of ancient Egyptian history, but she was especially revered in her hometown at Dendara. She was also the chief goddess at Edfu, a city she co-ruled with her husband, Horus.

The relief above comes from within the *pronaos* of the temple of Horus at Edfu and depicts Pharaoh offering Hathor—chief goddess of the district—a cache of soothing ointment.

Horus, son of Isis and spouse of Hathor, was one of the greatest gods of ancient Egypt and always surrounded by a bevy of potent female divinities eager to protect his territory.

This enormous statue of Horus in falcon-form, wearing the combined crowns of Upper and Lower Egypt, is one of two built to stand guard over the façade of his majestic temple at Edfu.

The goddess Nekhbet could sometimes take the form of a vast, white cosmic cow, but she was more familiarly depicted as a vulture. With her wings outstretched protectively, Nekhbet was one of the nation's most ancient divinities and symbolized the glory of Southern ("Upper") Egypt.

Associated with Hathor and the northern cobra-goddess, Wadjet, Nekhbet's great temple was found in the city of Nekheb. This ancient relief of the deity, its colors still vivid after nearly 4,000 years, is found in the Anubis-chapel at Queen Hatshepsut's temple in Deir el-Bahri.

Of all the great divine "families" in ancient Egyptian religion, the coupling of Ptah and Sekhmet was one of the most revered. Worshipped as part of this unit in the city of Memphis, Sekhmet was one of the most beloved-yet-feared of all deities.

Depicted as a woman with the stoic, noble features of a lioness, Sakhmet was said to represent the destructive powers of the sun and the annual flood that could sometimes bring plague and misery upon Egypt. At the same time, she was credited with great healing powers over all forms of illness. Her priests were valued for their knowledge of medicinal arts.

The famed "Peak of the West" remains a lonesome, almost eerie sight for some modern visitors to Egypt—just as it was for the ancients. Across the river from Thebes, it loomed over the west bank of the Nile and was said to protect the hidden royal tombs. This naturally formed peak resembles a pyramid and was thought to be the dwelling-place of the great goddess Mertseger.

Nicknamed "She Who Loves the Silence," Mertseger was envisioned as a woman with the head of a serpent and the disposition to use her magical powers against anyone who dared disturb the resting places of the buried kings and queens.

Above is the first pylon of the famed temple of Isis on the island of Philae, in the First Cataract region of the Nile, near Aswan. One of ancient Egypt's greatest cult-centers and places of pilgrimage, the temple was also the last bastion of the old religion—closed only in the year 535 CE at the behest of the Emperor Justinian.

Today, thousands of visitors flock to the island every year, to gaze in wonder at the collection of shrines that were dismantled, relocated, and ultimately saved from flood waters in the 1970s. The island also features little temples dedicated to Hathor, Horus, and Imhotep. Isis, however, remains the chief attraction, and her image can be found throughout these stunningly well-preserved sanctuaries.

Isis is here depicted on a temple wall at Philae in front of her constant companion and devoted sister, the goddess Nephthys. Both goddesses are crowned with the cow's horns surrounding the solar-disc, indicating their status as chief deities and nurturers of the king.

Nephthys was the supporter of Isis and Osiris in all of their difficulties. In thanks for her powerful acts of loyalty and protection, she was particularly worshipped by the ancient Egyptians at Komir and Diospolis Parva.

Popularly known as the Kiosk of Trajan, this stunning architectural achievement was built on the Island of Philae to serve as a temporary protective "house" of the Sacred Bark of Isis when it returned to the island from various excursions.

Today, visitors to Philae will marvel at the beautiful symmetry of columns in this unique shrine and, if so disposed, linger into the evening for a spectacular laser light-show and tour through the various monuments.

Stalwart sphinx-images, built in Greco-Roman times, stand guard before the gateway of the first pylon of Isis's temple at Philae. On either side of the main entrance can be seen Coptic Christian crosses carved into the sandstone after the shrine was converted into a church in the 6th Century CE.

Beyond this monumental doorway we get a glimpse of the second pylon of this illustrious temple, which leads to a splendid hypostyle hall and the inner sanctum that once housed the cult-statue of the goddess.

A more complete view of the second pylon of the temple of Isis at Philae. On the right side of the pylon we see Pharaoh offering to Horus and his consort, Hathor, while on the left offerings are made to Osiris and Isis, whose images were defaced in antiquity. In the register above, the other gods of the temple are honored, including Nephthys, Nut, and Geb.

The great god Hapy (here portrayed in his "double" form) was one of the oldest and most hallowed deities along the Nile. Envisioned with both male and female attributes, Hapy was closely associated with the goddess Nekhbet and was considered to be the very embodiment (if not the source) of the Nile inundation. This exquisite relief comes from the temple at Luxor.

Hathor remained the quintessential goddess of beauty and joy throughout ancient Egyptian history. Here she appears in all of her elegance on the walls of the dual temple of Sobek and Haroeris at Kom Ombo in Upper Egypt. In that locale, Hathor formed part of one of the resident triads, as consort of crocodilian Sobek.

Short Bibliography

The following publications and journals were among those particularly helpful during the course of research. The reader is encouraged to explore all manner of books concerning ancient Egypt in order to satisfy the curiosity that *this* book hopefully inspires by its necessarily *incomplete* portrait of the goddesses.

Les Bulletins de l'Institut Francais d'Archeologie Orientale
Les Bulletins 1950-2006

Ptolemaic Philae
Eleni Vassilika, Orientalia Lovaniensia Analecta, Uitgeverij Peeters, Leuven 1989

Goddess Sites
Anneli S. Rufus and Kristan Lawson, Harper San Francisco, 1991

Studies in Pharaonic Society and Religion for J. Gwynn Griffiths
Occasional Publications 1991

Topographical Bibliography of Ancient Egyptian Texts, Reliefs, and Paintings, VI, Upper Egyptian Temples
Bertha Porter and Rosalind Moss, Griffith Institute, Asmolean Museum, Oxford, 1939

A Ptolemaic Lexikon: A Lexicographical Study of the Texts in the Temple of Edfu
Penelope Wilson, OLA Peeters, 1997
Egyptian Antiquities in the Nile Valley
James Baikie, Methuen & Co. LTD 1932
Lexikon der Agyptologie
Wolfgang Helck und Everhard Otto (Editors) **All Volumes**, Wiesbaden 1975-1986
Neter Dieux d'Egypte
Stephane Rossini and Ruth Schumann-Antelme (Preface de Christiane Desroches-Noblecourt) Editions Trismegiste, 1992
Les Pretres de l' ancienne Egypte
Serge Sauneron, Editions du Seuil, 1998
The Temple in Ancient Egypt: New Discoveries and Recent Research
Edited by Stephen Quirke, The Trustees of the British Museum, British Museum Press, 1997

The Night-Bark of Ra courses through the heavens. The goddesses Nekhbet and Wadjet stand guard above the old god's brow, Set and Wepwawet are on hand, and Nephthys scans the stars for signs of trouble. Meanwhile, the dreaded serpent Apophis writhes closer…

www.ingramcontent.com/pod-product-compliance
Lightning Source LLC
LaVergne TN
LVHW091041080826
845145LV00002B/574
9780615258805